THE PICTORIAL GUIDE TO
DOG CARE

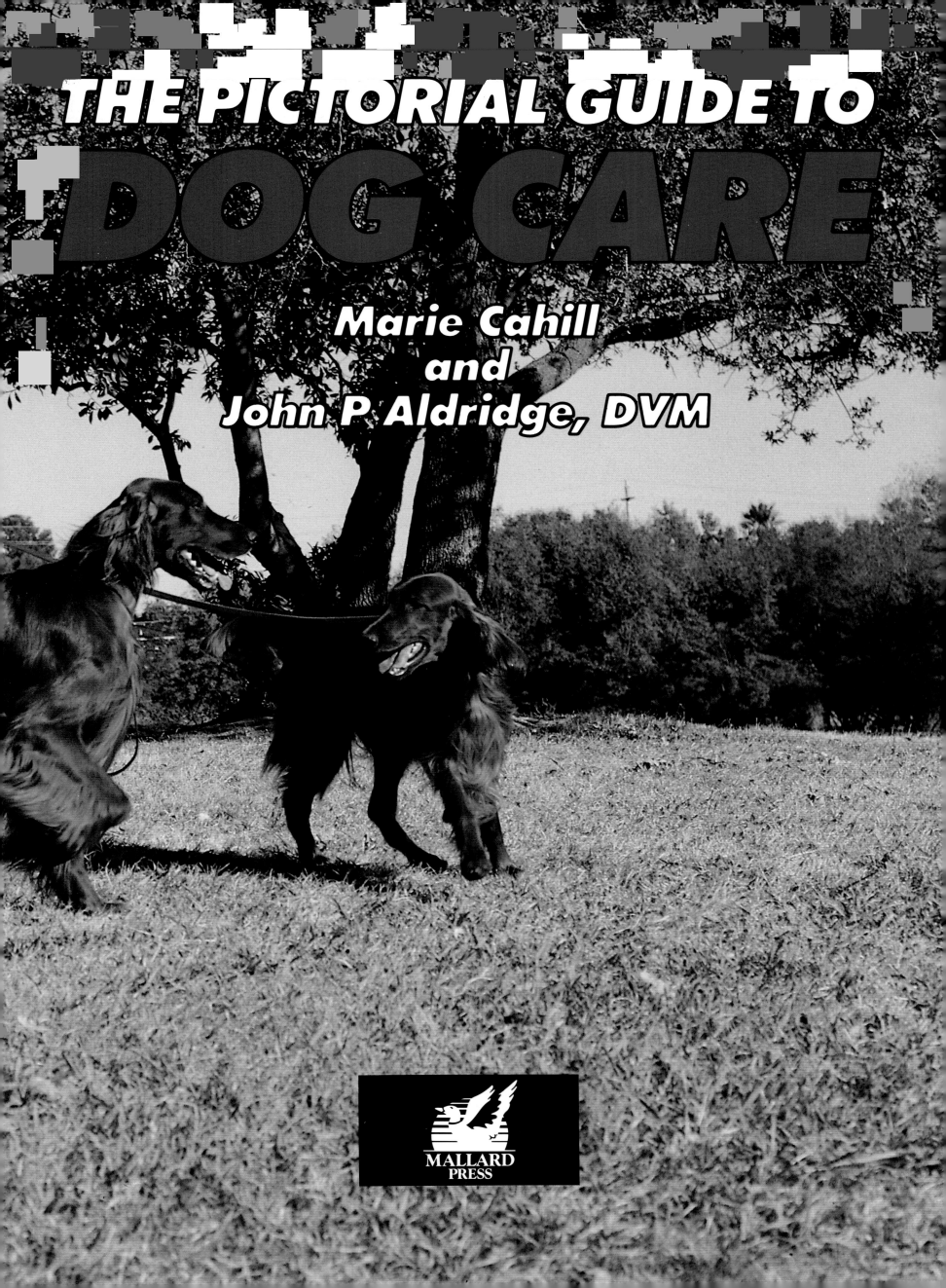

THE PICTORIAL GUIDE TO
DOG CARE

Marie Cahill
and
John P Aldridge, DVM

MALLARD
PRESS

First published in the United States of America in 1990 by The Mallard Press

Mallard Press and its accompanying design and logo are trademarks of BDD Promotional Book Company, Inc.

ISBN 0-792-45272-0

Printed in Hong Kong

Designed by Ruth DeJauregui

Captioned by Marie Cahill

Picture Credits

Page 1: A man and his best friend. Page 2-3: High-spirited Irish Setters need wide open spaces to work off their abundant energy.

Contents

Introduction

The dog is undoubtedly the oldest of the domesticated animals, and the early beginning of the canine race reaches far back into time. The more or less continuous association between man and dog began approximately in the Neolithic or Stone Age. Sufficient data have been collected to indicate that by this time, say 10,000 BC, the dog was utilized by man in solving his problems of existence. The Reindeer man of a preneolithic age was accompanied by the dog. The findings in the so-called kitchen middens along the coasts of Denmark and Scotland gave evidence of a Neolithic community in approximately 10,000 BC, in which the dog was the only domesticated animal. The remains of the lake dwellers of about 5000 BC in Switzerland indicate a similar association between dog and man.

The transition from the wild dog of the Eocene, who preyed on anything edible, to the helper of the Neolithic man was a slow process. It is quite within reason to suppose that the early wild dogs would prey on man as quickly as on any other animal and man certainly had no scruples about eating the wild dog if the opportunity offered. During the age of the cave man, which preceded the Neolithic, the relations between wild dog and man were anything but friendly. Some basis of understanding probably was developed during the time of the later cave man, who utilized the wild dog's power of scent and ability to procure food for his own purpose. Since both the wild dog and early man were flesh eaters, their interests in life were identical: securing an adequate food supply by killing other animals.

Man's reasoning powers, poor as they were, decided that he would benefit by an association with the wild dog. By so doing he would remove at least one enemy from his list and provide himself with a hunting ally, and a protector as well. This era was the beginning of mankind's friendship with the dog, and thus the dog was a powerful force in the advancement of civilization. The period of time necessary to consummate such an understanding was, no doubt, great, and we can imagine that it was accomplished by following the line of the least resistance. This would naturally involve finding wild dog puppies and rearing them in the caves. These, when grown, would be less wild than their parents and succeeding offspring would be still more amenable to such a relationship.

In this manner a better feeling for man developed in the dog. Darwin has pointed out that natural instincts are lost under domestication and new ones acquired, and we may assume that during this period the animal's instinctive hatred for man was slowly replaced by one of love. A gradual metamorphosis took place in the dog's reaction to its new mode of living, and by the advent of the later Neolithic man the dog could be depended upon for other things besides hunting for food. Its talents were diverted into other channels—protecting

***Facing page:* Since prehistoric times, the dog has been 'one of the family,' and today that family may well include lovebirds and kittens.**

sheep, cattle, and goats from predators and guarding the home as well as its master.

At this time there was no particular need for a specialized form, but these dogs had already undergone some variation in conformation and characteristics. Any early departures from the form of the common ancestor were probably not deliberate, but represented natural variations under domestication. As the problems of an increased culture became more complex, man often found it necessary for practical purposes to alter the conformation of his dogs. The animal thus progressed from the stage of unconscious variation to one of deliberate change.

There is no doubt that the early breeds bore a strong resemblance to some of the present breeds, but the only direct proof of this is found in the tracings on the walls of caves and the carvings of the Assyrian and Egyptian civilizations. A tablet in the British Museum, taken from the ruins of Nineveh, depicts an Assyrian hunting scene 2,500 years ago in which the dogs used are similar in form to the Mastiff and Great Dane of today. Egyptian figures of greater antiquity show dogs of the greyhound type, such as the Saluki of today. The Saluki is probably one of the oldest pure breeds and was used in ancient Persia for hunting the gazelle; it is not improbable that the dog's ancestry dates back to some of the scenes shown.

As far as the distribution of the early dog is concerned, there was no frontier; there is evidence that wherever man wandered his dog accompanied him. As a result, we have an animal whose breeds are scattered over the world and have adapted themselves perfectly to every environment. The form of the dog peculiar to any given region would be modified by the climate and type of the country in which the animal was used.

A brief survey of mythology and folklore shows that the sentiment of humans of an early period toward the canine family ran to extremes, and the dog was either despised or exalted to ridiculous heights. There are remarkably few references to the dog in the Bible, and the first mention concerns the Israelites in Egypt.

In ancient Egypt the dog was a symbol of divinity and its figure appears on temple decorations. According to Herodotus, when a dog died, the members of the family shaved—the usual expression of mourning. The feeling for the dog of that period is not, however, without some logical basis, for they believed that the appearance of the dog star Sirius was responsible for the overflowing of the Nile, with its resultant fertilizing effect on the inundated lands.

Pythagoras, coming from Egypt in the sixth century BC, founded in Greece and Italy a sect whose belief was that animals received the human soul after the death of the body. The dog was thought to be the favorite recipient, and the chief

At top: The Greyhound dates back to the time of the Ancient Egyptians, some 6000 years ago. *Facing page:* This Saluki puppy also has a long heritage, but authorities debate which breed can claim the distinction of being the oldest breed of dog. *Above:* The Neapolitan Mastiff is thought to be descended from the war dogs of ancient Rome. Its reputation for bravery and fierceness is well deserved, and today it works as a guard dog for the Italian police and armed forces. *Right:* Modern-day hunting dogs still retain the scenting abilities that made them indispensable to early man.

THE PICTORIAL GUIDE TO DOG CARE

disciples, when dying, were directed to breathe into the mouth of a dog. In Ethiopia, this veneration was carried to the absurd limits of electing a dog as king and the management of state affairs depended upon the interpretation of his barking.

Folklore abounds with references and each nation has its own reasons for commending their respective dogs. The Spanish dogs, bloodhounds, supposedly helped in conquering Peru and Mexico. The mastiffs of the Knights of Rhodes were highly thought of for their olfactory sense. St Eustace was regarded as the patron of dogs in southern Europe and St Hubert for dogs in northern Europe; the latter was called upon to cure cases of rabies.

Today, the association between man and his dog is as perfect as such a relationship can be. We have come to depend on it for numerous things, material and otherwise. Its assistance to man in gaining a livelihood, while often important, is negligible when we consider the partnership in a broader sense. The dog's popularity must be based on something more than mere utility, for there are other domestic animals of far greater economic importance, yet are never thought of in the same terms as the dog.

The dog has an almost universal appeal to members of the human family regardless of geographical location, age and position in the social scale. It fits into the hovel as well as the mansion and asks but one thing—human companionship. The normal dog gives its affection and loyalty and recognizes in the person of the master the center of its own particular universe.

The protective instinct is a part of the dog's very fiber, and history has recorded countless tales of dogs risking their lives for their masters. Certain breeds are better known for this trait than others, and while we associate the protection and preservation of human life with members of the larger breeds, it is an instinct common to all. In war time, the dog has been by man's side and carried on with a faithfulness that was blind to all danger.

The role of guardian of the premises is one the dog assumes naturally, for it has served as protector of the hearth since the cave-man era. A mute but impressive reminder of this fact takes us back into the ruins of Pompeii, destroyed in the first century AD. In the doorway of an excavated home is the figure of a dog in mosaic with the inscription: 'Cave Canen'—beware of the dog. After almost two thousand years of improvement in everything that man does he still relies on the protective instinct of the dog and uses the same words of warning to the stranger. The smallest dog resents intrusion into its master's domain in the same degree shown by its larger brother. What the dog may lack in size is compensated for by the determination with which it asserts itself.

Each and every dog is an individual entity and differs in some respect from every other member of the same breed as well as from dogs of other breeds. There are, to be sure, certain general reactions that are to be expected of practically all dogs as fairly characteristic of the canine family, but the finer mental processes resulting in differences in behavior vary with the individual dog. The behavior of dogs may be rated in the same plane with that of humans. Dogs show jealousy, anger, fear, affection and shame as common qualities; the more sensitive have moods as well. The indefinable bond that exists between dog and man is mirrored to a great degree in the eyes of the dog, and while it baffles description it is there for those who wish to see it.

Dogs are such wonderful companions that they are found in all places—from the snows of the Northeastern United States *(at top)* to the deserts of the Southwest *(right)*. *Above:* A friendly dog peeks his head inside the door, as if to ask, 'Can you come out and play?' *Facing page:* A page from everyone's childhood memories—the boy next door frolicking with his dog. *Overleaf:* A pair of Bichon Frisés and their adorable offspring.

THE PICTORIAL GUIDE TO DOG CARE

Breeds Of Dogs

Over 140 breeds are recognized by the American Kennel Club. They are divided into sporting dogs, hounds, working dogs, herding dogs, terriers, toys, non-sporting dogs and miscellaneous. In England the non-sporting group goes by the name 'Utility.' The members of each group have certain characteristics common to their respective class but each breed is a distinct unit with unique characteristics and temperaments.

Sporting Dogs

This group includes Pointer, German Shorthaired Pointer, Wirehaired Pointing Griffon, Chesapeake Bay Retriever, Flat-coated Retriever, Curly-coated Retriever, Golden Retriever, Labrador Retriever, English Setter, Irish Setter, Gordon Setter, Britanny Spaniel, Clumber Spaniel, Cocker Spaniel, English Springer Spaniel, Field Spaniel, Irish Water Spaniel, Sussex Spaniel and Welsh Springer Spaniel.

The Chesapeake Bays, water spaniels and retrievers are used almost entirely for bringing in waterfowl, although some of the retrievers are effective for upland game. The pointers and setters (English, Irish and Gordon) are used to find such birds as grouse, quail and pheasant, which they locate from body scent taken from the air. The work is performed in a beautiful fashion, impressive to watch. They range wide and freeze to a point when the game is located. Hunting ability is instinctive but a certain amount of training is desirable to bring the animal to perfection. The poise shown by a well-bred pointer or setter when in action is a wonderful sight. Many of the dogs will retrieve the birds after they have been shot. The Wirehaired Pointing Griffon works in a fashion similar to that of a pointer and, protected by its shaggy coat, is especially good in rough country.

The spaniels are good for birds and other small game, taking the scent from the ground and working differently from pointers and setters. The spaniels work with eyes and nose to the ground and usually in country where the larger bird dogs cannot get through as easily. When close to the quarry, the spaniel's tail moves quickly, with the exception of the Brittany Spaniel, which points its game. Being low to the ground spaniels can negotiate dense cover. The larger ones, such as the Clumber, work more slowly than the smaller ones, such as the Cocker. The Cocker is by far the most popular of the group, with the English Springer next. They will all retrieve and take to the water, the larger ones having an advantage in this element. The recent interest shown in field trials for spaniels indicate a healthy regard for this group. Incidentally, field trials for any of the

Facing page: **A boy and his German Shorthaired Pointer. These hardy dogs need plenty of exercise.**

THE PICTORIAL GUIDE TO DOG CARE

At top: Two youngsters—a small boy and his Cocker Spaniel puppy. **Above:** English Springer Spaniels are robust dogs that enjoy a good, long romp with their owners. **Facing page:** Labrador Retrievers are extremely intelligent animals—some even attempt to play the organ!

sporting dogs give us an idea of an animal's performance under working conditions and should be considered a supplement to his bench show record.

All weights and sizes given below are for males, which are somewhat taller and heavier than the females of the same breed. Chesapeake Bays will scale from 60 to 75 pounds and measure 23 to 26 inches at the shoulders. The retrievers are about the same weight but generally somewhat shorter. English Setters run from 40 to 45 pounds and about 22 inches in height. The Pointer and the other setters vary some from this weight and size. The Clumber Spaniel is the heaviest of the spaniels, weighing as much as 65 pounds in some cases; the Springer runs to about 45 pounds, and the Cocker, the smallest, between 18 and 24.

None in this group has cropped ears and all have weather-resisting coats, with the exception of the pointer. The dogs in this sporting group find the game and retrieve it, but the hunter must kill it. The history of sporting dogs, particularly in early times, is probably more complete than that of almost any other group. These dogs were used by the wealthier class and early authors, especially the English, devoted much time and effort to give accurate descriptions of hunting breeds and hunting conditions. Since the dogs were bred and used for hunting and sporting purposes it necessarily follows that they have been man's companions under most conditions. The outstanding characteristics of the group are a gentle nature and lovable disposition. Their devotion, dependability, and quiet manner make them ideal pets and companions. They are possessed of great common sense and are reserved or spirited as the occasion or the master's mood dictates. Members of this group are used in many instances as pets only and the recent great popularity of the spaniel, particularly the Cocker, is a tribute to its adaptability as an all-round dog. According to the American Kennel Club's 1988 annual list of the most popular dogs in the United States, the Cocker Spaniel ranked first, the Labrador Retriever was second and the Golden Retriever, fourth.

Above: The thick, rough and oily coat of the Otter Hound is made to repel water. **Facing page, above:** The Beagle is equally adapted to the field as it is to the living room. Beagles make fine pets, but they have a tendency to be stubborn and may require obedience training. **Facing page, below:** The Bloodhound's scenting ability is legendary. Long-esteemed by the aristocracy, the breed probably takes its name from its royal connections as much as from its skill at hunting. The 'blood' in Bloodhound certainly has no connection with the ferocious, for this is one of the gentlest of breeds.

Hounds

This group is comprised of the following: Afghan Hound, Basset Hound, Beagle, Bloodhound, Dachshund (three varieties), Scottish Deerhound, American Foxhound, English Foxhound, Greyhound, Harrier, Norwegian Elkhound, Otter Hound, Saluki, Whippet, Irish Wolfhound, Russian Wolfhound, Basenji, Black and Tan Coonhound, Borzoi, Ibizan Hound, Pharaoh Hound and Rhodesian Ridgeback.

Some of the oldest members of the canine family belong to this group. Research in art and writings has established the fact that hounds came from the East. The Saluki, or gazelle hound, came from Persia and its conformation today is almost the same as that shown in the earliest pictures available. Hounds hunt by either sight or scent and most of them kill their quarry. The Greyhound, Wolfhound, and Deerhound are examples of those hunting by sight; the Basset, Beagle, Blood, Fox, Harrier, Otter and Elk locate the quarry by scent.

The Afghan Hound resembles the Saluki in conformation but has an entirely different and unique distribution of hair—the back, sides of neck and face are sparsely covered, and the rest of the body has thick, silky hair. The Whippet is a modified Greyhound developed entirely for racing although the breed is used considerably as a pet. The Greyhound was bred for coursing the hare and is used extensively for racing. It shows the most correct form for speed in the entire dog world, combining stamina and suppleness in perfect proportion. The Greyhound stands as a tribute to fine breeding for a specialized purpose that has never been lost sight of over a period of centuries. The original purpose of the

wolfhounds is apparent from their name, but at present they are used almost entirely as companions and guardians. The Russian Wolfhound, an aristocrat in bearing and appearance, would grace any castle. The Irish Wolfhound is thought of more in its original capacity; the tallest breed of dog and capable of taking the back of a wolf in its mouth, it is exceedingly gentle and tractable. These big fellows should have plenty of room to stretch their legs.

Harriers are used to hunt hares; Beagles and Bassets are smaller hounds used for hares and rabbits. These three breeds hunt in packs. Beagles make lively little companions and are popular as house pets. The names of Foxhounds, Deerhound, Elkhound, and Otterhound are descriptive of their work. The Norwegian Elkhound is more often seen as a pet than are the others named. The Otterhound may claim some fame as one of the ancestors of the Airedale. The Bloodhound is famous for its remarkable olfactory development and was used for tracking criminals. This is probably the oldest breed of the sporting dogs that hunt by scent. The sanguinary name is misleading, for Bloodhounds are quite gentle and possess the saddest face in dogdom. The Dachshund is also popular as a house pet, being a vivacious little fellow with lots of character. Bred for hunting badgers and foxes, it is the only hound that will dig in. It is of German origin and comes in three varieties: smooth, wire and long haired; the first is most widely seen and best known.

There are no cropped ears in this group; the Elkhound is the only one having upright ears. The coats vary from the smooth, close type of the Greyhound to the long, silky kind seen on the Afghan Hound. In size there is also a wide range, from the Irish Wolfhound of 120 pounds to the Dachshund of about 15.

Working Dogs

The working dog group consists of dogs which are or have been at some time useful to man in his daily life. We associate them with the more practical aspects of our daily life, although their original purpose in life is mostly overlooked today. They have all been developed for some definite purpose and, in their ability to perform certain work, are as specialized as are the sporting dogs for their own duties. They are excellent guardians of person and property. The fearlessness so characteristic of the canine family reaches a high peak in these dogs, and their usefulness as protectors is enhanced by an impressive size. Centuries of assistance to man in his work have imbued the group with a sense of responsibility which is reflected in their manner.

The Doberman, Rottweiler, Giant Schnauzer and Boxer are of German origin and served primarily as guardians for farms, and the last two are sometimes referred to as 'butcher dogs'—guardians of butchers' wagons. They all have docked tails and the Schnauzer and Doberman have cropped ears as well. They retain to a marked degree the traits which have made them valuable in the past: aggressive when necessary; gentle and devoted companions to their masters. The Doberman is the most popular of the trio, being especially keen and highly intelligent. This is a short-coated dog of sleek beauty who has gained a host of friends and admirers by its unassuming manner and protective qualities. The Doberman is particularly adapted to training and is used extensively for police work. Boxers have docked tails and cropped ears. They are of good size—up to about 24 inches for males—stocky, fearless and make good companions and guardians. The Boxer is businesslike without being obtrusive, and its short, usually brindle-colored coat is easily cared for.

The Mastiff and Bull Mastiff fall properly within the group of guardians, for they assume this work naturally. Both are huge, short-coated dogs of fawn or brindle color with black mask and ears. In spite of their muscular development, they have an aristocrat bearing, and though thoroughly formidable if the need arises, complete docility has endeared them to the hearts of many. The Mastiff is the oldest of the British dogs. It has been said that they were found in England by the Roman invaders, who took them back to fight lions in the arenas. In the Elizabethan period they were kept to bait bears and lions; the rules of this so-called sport required three Mastiffs to be sent against a bear and four against a lion. The Bull Mastiff comes from a Bulldog-Mastiff cross.

The most popular of the large guardian dogs is the Great Dane. This huge, regal-looking animal should never be less than 30 inches high and comes in fawn, brindle, blue and harlequin. For centuries the Dane was bred for wild-boar hunting and had also been used to some extent for draft purposes, while today it is considered most effective and valuable as companion and protector. It is short coated and has cropped ears.

The Doberman is named for the man who developed the breed— Louis Dobermann. Dobermans in the United States have cropped ears; those in Great Britain, like the 'Dobe' *at top* do not.

People throughout the far northern reaches of the world have developed breeds able to withstand the harsh cold of the arctic. *Above:* A West Siberian Laika, flanked by two Gontjaja harnessed to a sledge. The Gontjaja, of which there are several varieties, is one of the most popular dogs in the Soviet Union. *Right:* The Eskimo Dog, another breed that pulls sledges in the arctic, is also used for rescuing avalanche victims. *Facing page, above:* The Kuvasz has been a guard dog, a sheep dog, and a hunter of wild boar. Its friendly temperament makes it a fine companion as well. *Facing page, below:* The New-foundland is as much at home in the water as it is on dry land.

THE PICTORIAL GUIDE TO DOG CARE

The Newfoundland and St Bernard are old breeds and have a very colorful background. The saving of human life is more or less instinctive in any breed, but it has probably attained its highest form in these two breeds. The all-black and black-and-white Newfoundland and the red-and-white St Bernard have, in common, a dignified bearing and a gentle, unruffled manner. Their facial expression reveals sagacity and kindness. The Eskimo, Siberian Husky, Alaskan Malamute and Samoyed are the dogs that man depends upon in the snow and ice of the arctic and antarctic. They are sledge dogs, although in northern Siberia the Samoyed is used to herd reindeer for the Samoyed tribes. The group is characterized by compactness, muscular development and heavy coat. Their coloring runs to any of the accepted dog colors with the exception of the Samoyed who must be white, white and biscuit or cream. The Eskimo and Alaskan Malamute will scale as much as 85 pounds, the Siberian husky up to 64 pounds, and the Samoyed 55 pounds as a maximum.

The Great Pyrenees is a large, white dog from the Pyrenees; some are as large as Great Danes. The Kuvasz comes from Hungary and is large, white and beautiful. It is sometimes called the Hungarian Sheepdog, although this is somewhat misleading as there are two other breeds of sheep dogs in Hungary: the Komondor and Puli.

BREEDS OF DOGS

Herding Dogs

Developed for their herding abilities, the members of this group are intelligent and show a resourcefulness which enables them to work out the solution of problems without the aid of their masters. Centuries of care given to their charges has given these dogs a splendid sense of dependability and devotion. They make devoted pets and are to be recommended where proper environment can be provided.

The Collie is probably the best known of the sheepherding dogs and comes in two forms: rough coated and smooth, although the latter is not so commonly seen. The Shetland Sheepdog is, in effect, a miniature rough Collie and possesses the same temperament. It is popular with those who admire the Collie but wish a smaller dog having the Collie qualities. The Old English Sheepdog is the shaggy coated, bobtailed animal of distinctive appearance, originally bred for cold climates. Its ambling gait and conformation somehow suggest a bear. The breed is most gentle and affectionate.

The German Shepherd scarcely needs a description. This is a general all-round dog—herding was its original work, but its performance in war and police work have brought it to the attention of the world. An immense popularity for the breed followed World War II and it is still quite a favorite. The Belgian shepherd dogs resemble in many respects the German Shepherd. The three breeds are the Belgian Malinois, Belgian Tervueren and the Belgian Groenendael, the most well known of the three. The Bouvier des Flandres is another breed of Belgian sheepherder and general farm dog. It is taller than the other Belgian dogs and has cropped ears and tail. The Briard is an old breed of French farm dog used in many ways and is about the same size as the Bouvier.

The Welsh Corgi is classed with the herding dogs, although its real job was to repel animals trespassing its master's domain. This is the smallest of the group, measuring about 12 inches at the shoulder. There are two recognized forms of the breed: Pembroke Welsh Corgi and Cardigan Welsh Corgi. The most readily discernible difference to the average person is in the tails of these dogs: the Pembroke variety has a short tail; the Cardigan has a long one similar to a fox's. Both dogs have a foxy appearance.

At top: Queen Elizabeth as a child in July 1936, with her mother and her pet Corgis. *Above:* Erwin Jensen, a German soldier and his dog, Dino, on guard duty. *Right:* Private Ole Sorensen of the Danish Army and King on patrol. *Facing page:* A beautiful Collie.

THE PICTORIAL GUIDE TO DOG CARE

At top: The perky West Highland White Terrier is a popular pet. *Above:* The coat of the Kerry Blue Terrier is soft, dense and wavy. Like Poodles, these dogs do not shed, but the coat needs clipping every six to eight weeks. *Facing page, above:* A boy and his American Staffordshire Terrier. These courageous dogs are very gentle with people. *Facing page, below:* The Welsh Terrier, like all terriers, is a very energetic dog.

Terriers

This group comprises twenty-five breeds whose purpose in life is to rid the world of vermin or anything apt to prove a nuisance to man—rats, badgers, woodchucks, foxes, otters and so on. The larger members of the group, such as the Airedale, have been used against large game—grizzly bears and lions.

Terriers may be described as medium in size, with a few exceptions, and having in common courage and a determination to see a job through even in the face of death. A terrier must be wiry and tough and must never back out of anything. The dogs are lithe, fast, and have solid muscle and good bone development. The heads, legs and coat are all-important structures. The jaws are powerful, with large teeth that approximate evenly to facilitate biting and holding the quarry. The legs must be strong, with firm feet and tough nails in case it is necessary to dig in—or 'go to earth,' as the expression goes. In most terriers the coat is short, close and able to resist both wear and weather. In addition to all the requisites of conformation, this dog must possess the all-important terrier character inherent in the dog's very fiber—spirit and grit. These dogs make excellent pets and companions, for they are mostly of a suitable size for small quarters, whether in or out of town; they have an engaging personality; and their lively manner makes them interesting to have about.

Great Britain is responsible for most of the terrier breeds and terriers existed in many parts of the British Isles for hundreds of years, doing the work expected of them but seldom attracting much notice. It was the sporting dog that came in for the honors in early times. It is believed that mongrel hound blood was the first basis for terrier strains. The native English terrier of centuries back may be considered to have been nondescript compared to the present-day dog, but it was probably the basic stock for the now existing English terriers.

It was not until the nineteenth century that certain members of the group began to be bred according to preconceived ideas and the resulting progeny assumed a new importance. However, some authorities believes that the Scottish terriers were bred in form more nearly like the present varieties for many years before being taken up outside their home environs.

Some of the terriers have docked tails and four breeds have cropped ears. In conformation the terriers may be regarded roughly according to their place of origin, although the innate characteristics are common to the group.

The Scotch dogs—Cairn, Scotty, Skye, and West Highland White Terrier—are compact in form and have fairly short legs. They have the strong weather-resisting coats that one would expect in dogs from that part of the world. There is reason to believe that a common parent stock is responsible for all of them.

The Cairn is a lively little terrier, very intelligent. The Scotty is a debonair fellow who has gone far in his travels from his native Highlands. The breed needs no introduction or description, for we see its picture in all forms of advertising matter. The West Highland White is a lively and charming fellow, popular in both the show ring and as a pet. The Skye is a determined, fighting terrier greatly misjudged because of its long, flowing coat. The breed was popular in the late nineteenth century, but today is not as well known as the others.

THE PICTORIAL GUIDE TO DOG CARE

The terriers of the Border country—Dandie Dinmont, Bedlington, and Border—enjoy popularity in the Great Britain, but less so in the United States. The Dandie and the Bedlington share the honors for being the oddest-looking dogs in the terrier group. The Bedlington is described as having a lamblike appearance, but is one of the gamest dogs alive. The Dandie Dinmont, quite low in front and high in the stern, is considered an ancestor of the Bedlington. Sir Walter Scott mentions Dandie Dinmont in *Guy Mannering* and this fact is supposed to be responsible for the dog's recognition as a breed. Border terriers, though small, are hardy and spunky.

The English terriers include the Smooth Fox Terrier, Wire Fox Terrier, Bull Terrier, Airedale, Manchester Terrier and Lakeland Terrier. The fox terriers are old dogs, but the days of their popularity are passed. They symbolize all the necessary terrier qualities and did much to stimulate interest in the terrier group. The Wire Fox is the rough, broken-haired specimen, and is otherwise the same as the Smooth. The temperaments are supposed to be the same but the Wire is credited with having more personality. The Airedale is one of the largest of the terriers and one of the most businesslike. It weighs as much as 45 pounds of compact muscle, and is often used as a guardian dog as well as for hunting big game in the Rockies and in Africa. The Manchester is a smooth-coated, clean-looking black and tan terrier. The Bull Terrier possesses indomitable courage. They are no longer used as pit fighting dogs but the old spirit still prevails. Bull Terriers make excellent guardians, especially for children. The Lakeland is also from the British Isles and is of average terrier size. The Emerald Isle gives us the Irish Terrier, a red-coated bundle of scrappiness and dependable devotion, which makes a fine all-around dog. The Kerry Blue comes from the same country and boasts an unquenchable spirit. The Welsh Terrier and the Sealyham come from Wales; the former has all the desirable terrier traits and looks like a small Airedale. Sealys are compact and hardy little fellows, quite low to the ground but lacking none of the essential terrier characteristics.

The Schnauzers, both standard and miniature sizes, come from Germany and are smaller packages of the Giant Schnauzer listed under the working dogs. The Standard Schnauzer makes a good, general companion and stands from about 17 to 20 inches. The Miniature has the same points, but is 6 inches smaller.

If size is a factor in making a terrier selection, it might be well to remember that few of the group weigh more than 25 pounds—only the Airedale, Irish, Kerry and Bull Terrier.

Toys

The members of this group are pets in every sense of the word and base their claim for attention on the comfort and satisfaction they render their masters. Close companionship with humans for many centuries has made them understanding, sympathetic and often intuitive. They are invariably pert, intelligent and self-assertive. Their size and beauty and apparent helplessness make them the recipients of considerable attention. In some cases this works to the detriment of the animal, as many dogs are petted and pampered to the breaking point and often thoroughly spoiled. Some have terrier instincts which they are prevented from indulging because of their size. They adapt themselves well to a home environment and can be kept where outdoor activities are necessarily limited. The toys have a charm and comprehension far out of proportion to their size and have given immeasurable pleasure to many thousands of people all over the world. Many of the toy breeds are miniature versions of other breeds. An Italian Greyhound is a miniature of the Greyhound. Manchester and Bull terriers are also found in the toy category. Weighing about 7 pounds, the Toy Manchesters are active and intelligent. Toy Poodles are bright little fellows weighing less than 12 pounds. They may be any solid color. Miniature Pinschers resemble the Doberman and weigh from 6 to 10 pounds. The English Toy Spaniels—a grouping of the Prince Charles, King Charles, Ruby and Blenheim spaniels into one class—vary from nine to 12 pounds. They are really miniature spaniels, beautiful and gentle, and make fine pets. The Japanese Chin is an active, interesting little fellow. Long, somewhat silky hair, of particolors, black and white, and red and white, adds to their beauty.

Maltese dogs are alert and fearless and should weigh less than 7 pounds—4 to 6 pounds is considered ideal. The long, white, silky coat reaches the ground and gives a striking appearance. The Papillon is an interesting little chap weighing under 9 pounds. Its large upright ears give the impression of butterfly wings and it is often called the 'butterfly dog.'

The Pug is of Chinese origin and is a gentle, lovable dog weighing from 14 to 18 pounds. The Pug's popularity has risen and declined with the whims of fashion, and today it is once again a favorite pet. The Pekingese, or Peke, is the aristocratic little lion dog from ancient China. It is one of the most popular members in the group and deserves this ranking by virtue of its courage and personality. If a little dog may be said to be imposing looking, then the term applies to the Peke. Pekes love to romp about and are to be considered active dogs.

The Pomeranian, from old Pomerania, runs a close second to the Peke in popularity, and is a vivacious, keen-minded animal. Its snappy action enables it to step out with the best of them and it makes a desirable pet. The Pomeranian is a beautiful dog in coat, coloring, and proportion.

Yorkshire Terriers, in spite of their long mantle of hair reaching to the ground, have sporting instincts. The silky coat of dark, steel-blue coloring gives them an outstanding appearance.

The Chihuahua and Mexican Hairless come from Mexico and both show terrier traits. The Chihuahua is very active and quite popular, and weighs from two to six pounds.

At top: Canine authorities are divided on whether the all-white Maltese originated on the island of Malta or in the Sicilian town of Melita. *Above:* The Chinese Crested Dog is one of the rare hairless breeds. Dogs born with hair, like the one on the right, are called powder puffs. *Right:* The Chihuahua is the smallest breed in the world. *Facing page:* Pugs are very affectionate and long to be part of the family. Grooming and exercise requirements are minimal, but Pugs love—and need—attention.

THE PICTORIAL GUIDE TO DOG CARE

At top: **Legend has it that the Schipperke is descended from two black, tailless dogs that reputedly saved William of Orange from an assassin.** *Above:* **Its heritage as a carriage dog — when it would race among the wheels — can easily be seen in the Dalmatian today, for this dog loves to run and requires plenty of exercise.** *Facing page:* **A Miniature Poodle and her puppy. Note the 'Puppy' clip on the youngster.**

Non-sporting Dogs

These dogs are used almost entirely as pets, companions and guardians. Some breeds have been transferred to this group since they are no longer used as primarily intended, such as the Bulldog.

The Boston Terrier claims the honor of being the American-bred dog. It is a clean-looking, short-coated, animated dog which adapts itself to any surroundings. The breed is divided into three classes; lightweight, under 15 pounds; middleweight, 15 to 20 pounds; and heavyweight, 20 to 25 pounds.

Bulldogs are gentle and thoroughly tractable despite their somewhat pugnacious facial expression and the history of their past activities. The breed was used for bull baiting in England; since that has been abolished, it has been used as pet, companion, and guardian. In this latter respect the Bulldog may be relied on completely. An outstanding characteristic is its tenacity of purpose — once committed to a thing, the dog is there for keeps. It is short coated, clean looking and weighs about 50 pounds.

Chow Chows — or just Chows, as they are often called — are of Chinese origin and are truly beautiful animals. The coat, mostly red or black, is quite abundant, with an ample ruff about the neck which accentuates the lionlike expression. The Chow is rather massive, although compact and solid. They are canine individualists and will not be pushed into things. The Dalmatian comes from Dalmatia and is the polka-dotted dog invariably seen in every firehouse in the days of horse-drawn apparatus. It weighs up to 50 pounds, is short coated, gentle and affectionate.

French Bulldogs are splendid, mild-mannered animals. They make good pets and guardians. Poodles are among the most popular dogs today. They are easily taught and their qualities make them all-around dogs. Poodles should weigh more than 20 pounds. Miniature Poodles are small editions of the large Poodles, and weigh under 20 pounds.

Schipperke, or Skip, is the barge dog of the canals of Holland and Belgium. This is an active, black-coated fellow from 6 to 18 pounds in weight. Its front presents a foxlike appearance, but it has just a stump of a tail. The Keeshond is a Dutch dog of very old breeding. A hardy breed with a good disposition, it looks like a large Pom, with a silver-gray coat with black-tipped hair. Lhasa Apsos originated in Central Asia and are members of a very old breed. They have a dense coat and vary in color from golden, through many different shades, to black.

THE PICTORIAL GUIDE TO DOG CARE

Choosing Your Dog

You have decided to get a dog. There are dozens of questions to be answered? Do you want a purebred or a mongrel; if a purebred, which breed is most suited to your needs? your home? your personality? Is the dog to be kept in the city or in the country? What is the best age and sex? Will it be a family dog—the companion of children and adults, or will it give all its time to one person? Where can you purchase the dog, and what about the reliability of the source?

You have every reason to be particular about this new member of the family, for it will occupy your home and thoughts, and a great deal of the satisfaction both pet and owner later experience from this association will depend on how these questions are decided.

Puppy or Adult?

The dog's age is usually one of the first considerations, and, for most people, the puppy is by far the best choice. With its cuddly appearance and personality, the puppy has a charm all its own. Its activity, irrepressible spirit and mischievousness are a joy to behold. Watching a puppy develop is more than just a biological affair—it is fascinating to note the puppy's reactions to various situations and how these reactions change with maturity.

For practical purposes it is better to get a young dog where there are children in the household. While most older dogs take readily to children in a new home, there are instances of a strained relationship at the beginning. Some adult dogs used to an environment of grownups are often bewildered by the antics of children and need a little time to adjust themselves. A child is not always a respecter of the canine sensibilities, and the growing puppy often learns to accept the playful roughhousing in better spirits than does its mature brother.

While a puppy does require training, the task is not difficult, providing the owner has the time and is consistent. On the other hand, one advantage of adopting an adult dog is that it is properly trained and housebroken (or should be). The adult dog is also past the illnesses and upsets that puppies are prone to.

***Facing page:* This young girl and her mixed breed dog will be loving companions for years to come. Though some people prefer a purebred dog, a mixed breed is just as agreeable a companion.**

At top: **When choosing a dog, most people find they cannot resist an adorable puppy—and sometimes people can't adopt just one.** *Above:* **Out for an afternoon swim.**

An older dog is good choice for the elderly person who desires the companionship of a dog but does not have the energy to take care of a puppy.

If you decide you want an adult dog, a good place to look is the local humane society. You can also contact local vets. They may know of a dog in need of a home. Sometimes people move and cannot take their dog with them; sometimes they decide they don't want the responsibility of a pet. If you want a purebred dog, contact local breeders. Breeders sometimes hold on to puppies for show purposes, but the puppies don't always turn out as expected. Breeders may also be looking for a home for the older female dog no longer used for breeding. Finally, breed societies often run rescue societies for dogs of their breed.

Male or Female?

Another important consideration is the sex of the dog. The female dog is less of a wanderer and is often the more easily trained and affectionate, and a female is certainly as dependable under working conditions. A female dog is inconvenient when she goes into heat, but unless you intend to breed her, it is best to have the dog spayed anyway. Many dog lovers insist on getting a female as a pet, but there will always be those who prefer the male's personality. Fans of the male dog believe the male has more character—which, depending on your point of view, is a plus or a minus. The male's independent nature may give it more character, but males seem to be harder to train and they do tend to roam.

The importance of neutering both males and females should not be overlooked. Unless the owner is dedicated to breeding show quality, purebred dogs, there is little justification for keeping the pet intact. Neutered dogs have fewer medical problems, are easier to care for and more stable in training and temperament. Most importantly, unwanted breedings do not contribute to the tragic pet overpopulation problem.

Purebred or Mongrel?

Should you get a purebred dog or a mixed breed dog? Many a family has adopted a mixed breed, or mongrel, puppy when the neighbor's dog produced an unplanned litter and has been completely happy with the newest addition to the family. The mongrel has given satisfaction in so many homes that its status as a pet is without question. The love and devotion a dog is capable of showing is, after all, independent of pedigree. The appearance of the nonpedigreed dog, at its worst, may be nondescript, but its charm is often so great that we completely lose sight of its exterior. The oddest-looking mongrel is not without a certain dignity of manner. In the mongrel's favor, it is less prone to the inherited diseases that a pedigreed dog may be subject to, and some authorities claim that mongrels seem less susceptible to common aliments. Finally, mongrels are often free or the price is nominal. Humane societies charge a fee, but in exchange many give you a certificate for vaccinating and neutering the dog at a reduced cost.

Many people prefer a purebred dog because its ancestry is a known quantity. You know what to expect in terms of size, appearance and personality; therefore, once you know you want a purebred dog, you then have to decide on the breed—which is a taste issue as well as a practical one. Maybe you want a Collie, but do you have the time to groom it and give it the exercise it needs? Different breeds have distinct temperaments: Labs are known for their good-natured personalities; Beagles, while cheerful, have a stubborn streak; Norwich Terriers, despite their diminutive size, make good watchdogs. Find out what kind of breed is best suited for your personality. Read various books on different breeds, talk to people who own a breed that you are interested in.

The size of the breed is a practical consideration. Small and toy dogs typically require very little exercise and are a good choice for apartment dwellers.

At top: Shetland Sheepdogs are devoted to their families, but tend to be shy with other people and animals. *Above:* Two Dachshund puppies—waiting to be adopted.

However, that is not to say that the large dog cannot exist happily in the city, as long as it is given plenty of love, attention and exercise. Large dogs playing or strolling along with their owners are a common sight in city parks. Keep in mind, that although large dogs may make good watchdogs, they are expensive to buy as well as keep. The cost of feeding a Great Dane is considerably higher than that of a West Highland White Terrier. Large dogs, though quite often gentle-natured, are, simply by virtue of their size, difficult for young children and elderly people to handle.

When purchasing a purebred dog, it is best to go to a reliable breeder rather than a pet shop. Puppies in pet shops often come from unknown and therefore unreliable sources. Unfortunately, pet shop puppies may be bred from dogs in poor condition and are born weak. Their conditions can be aggravated by traveling long distances across the country. Breeders, on the other hand, are usually well established and depend upon satisfied customers for a continuance of their business. The American Kennel Club will furnish a list of approved breeders of any kind of dog for a given locality. Dog magazines also have lists of breeders. These magazines provide details about dog shows, which are fun to watch as well as a good source of information about the breed in general and the availability of puppies. In doing your research about the breed, be sure to find out whether that breed is prone to any hereditary diseases. If so, contact the breed society to find what is being done to eradicate the disease. The breed society can also tell how to obtain a dog that has been certified free of the disorder. Certification is important because these disorders cannot be detected at a young age. As far as the general health of the puppy is concerned, if you are buying your puppy from a reputable breeder, the puppy will be healthy. A good breeder won't sell an unhealthy puppy.

Once you have found a breeder with a litter, you will have to decide which puppy is right for you. This is a completely personal and subjective decision, but there are a few things to keep in mind. If you can, watch the puppies interact with each other. The sleeping puppy in the corner may have been romping around vigorously not two minutes before your arrival. The puppies' parents can provide a good clue to the pups' temperaments. A friendly and confident mom and dad are unlikely to produce a timid puppy.

At top: Dogs fit into all walks of life, as illustrated by this 1925 portrait of HRH the Prince of Wales (later King Edward VIII).
When choosing a dog, think about its size. The small puppy *above* could grow up to be a big dog, like the one *at right.* Do you have the time to exercise and the space needed for a big dog? *Facing page:* Dogs are social animals and love the company of humans.

THE PICTORIAL GUIDE TO DOG CARE

Caring For Your Puppy

Anyone who has ever owned a puppy will agree that puppies are absolutely adorable creatures. They are also a lot of work. In many ways, a new puppy is like a new baby. Puppies require an unbelievable amount of attention—turn away for just five seconds and your puppy will be chewing on your shoes or squatting on your Oriental rug. But most people find that the joys of owning a puppy far outweigh the mishaps.

The best time to adopt a new puppy is an important issue. Most authorities agree that the best time for the puppy to bond with its new owner is seven weeks. Between eight and nine weeks, puppies experience the equivalent of the 'fear period' seen in infants of eight months.

Before you bring your puppy home, your house should be ready for the new arrival. Make sure the area is warm enough for the size dog and the time of year and weather conditions. Away from the warmth of the nest, young puppies are vulnerable to hypothermia, or abnormal chilling. A place to sleep, such as a cardboard box or half of a pet carrier, gives your puppy an important sense of security. For the last seven weeks, the young puppy has been surrounded by its mother, brother and sisters. Having its own territory will ease the transition to the strange, new environment. Your puppy will also need food and water bowls as well as a lightweight collar and leash.

In addition, your house should be 'puppy-proofed.' A tiny puppy can hurt itself if it should fall down a flight of stairs, so barricade stairways or be prepared to keep a close eye on the puppy. Because puppies love to chew, keep electrical cords out of their way. Puppies also have a fondness for shoes, so keep closet doors closed. Make sure your puppy doesn't have access to poisons—cleaners, paints, insecticides.

Outside, make sure the puppy can't get out of the yard. Conversely, make sure other dogs can't get in. If possible, fence off a small section off the yard—a young puppy will have a greater sense of security if it is confined in a smaller area as opposed to having the run of the yard.

Facing page: **It's hard to believe that this tiny puppy will grow up to be a sleek, powerful Doberman. At this tender age, a puppy needs plenty of warmth because its body does not conduct heat well, so make sure that your new puppy's bed is in an area free from drafts.**

Training Your Puppy

The first—and easiest—lesson your puppy will need to learn is its name. If you always address your puppy by its name, it will soon respond. Avoid using nicknames that might confuse your puppy.

Next teach your puppy the meaning of the word 'NO.' Puppies are curious creatures and will want to explore their new surroundings. Your new puppy is bound to get into trouble sooner or later—it will want to chew on an electric cord or pounce on your cat or bite your toes.

Housebreaking Your Puppy

You can start housebreaking lessons as soon as you bring your puppy home. Take it outside to give it a chance to relieve itself—and then praise the puppy when it does. Most puppies should have the opportunity to relieve themselves every couple of hours and after every meal.

Many people paper train their dogs. This method works well for small dogs that are confined to an apartment for long hours at a time, but most people find that paper training is an extra step that is better to forego, particularly for larger breeds. A puppy that has been paper trained will have to be retrained to relieve itself outdoors.

The best way to housebreak your puppy is simply to keep an eye on it. When your puppy becomes restless, take it outdoors and praise it lavishly when it relieves itself. A good practice is to always go to the same spot so the puppy associates that particular spot with relieving itself. Using a simple command, while not necessary, reinforces the idea. Of course, you can't watch your dog every single minute of the day. Accidents are bound to happen, and when they do the puppy should be scolded and taken outside to the proper spot. Then praise it lavishly for being in the right place! Positive reinforcement (praise) works far faster than negative reinforcement (punishment).

Some trainers recommend putting the puppy in a cage, box or other small area when the owner is unable to keep a constant eye on the youngster. You will have to introduce your puppy to the cage, but once accustomed to the cage, most puppies will adjust to being left alone. The theory behind the cage is that most puppies will not dirty an area they are confined in. Once you let the puppy out of the cage, be sure to take it outside immediately.

If you take your puppy outside after every meal, first thing in the morning and last thing at night, it will be housebroken fairly soon. As with any kind of training, consistency is the key—establish a schedule and scold your puppy when it does wrong. Keep in mind, too, that an essential part of housebreaking depends on the owner. It's up to you to recognize the warning signs of a puppy about to relieve itself. Watch for sniffing the ground or circling the room. Feeding your puppy on a regular schedule aids housebreaking because it helps to regulate the puppy's digestive system.

At top: A trio of Rottweiler puppies. Above: This puppy will make this a Christmas to be remembered. Right: To paper train your puppy, you need to keep a constant eye on it. When your puppy becomes restless or circles, immediately place it on the newspaper—and then praise it for using the proper spot. Facing page: This new dog owner certainly has his hands full.

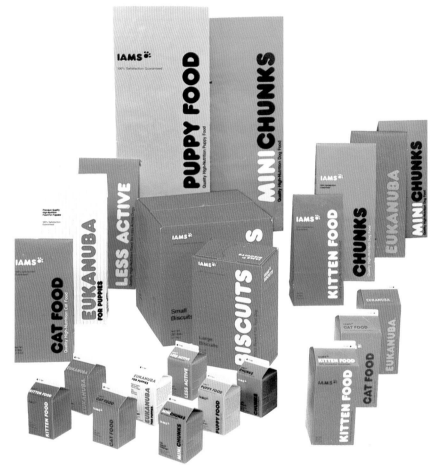

At top: Two young puppies exploring their new surroundings. *Above, right:* Feeding time. The amount of food needed varies greatly depending on the breed, but all puppies need about twice as much food for their weight as adult dogs do. *Above:* IAMS is one brand of premium pet food offering a specially formulated diet for puppies. *Facing page, above:* A girl and her new puppy. *Facing page, below:* Relaxing in the backyard. Make sure your backyard is puppy-proofed—no holes in the fence where a small puppy could crawl through.

Feeding Your Puppy

A puppy requires twice the nutrients per body weight as an adult dog. Protein, which is essential for growth, is a vital element during the first year of a dog's life. High-quality commercial puppy foods formulated to meet a puppy's needs are now available. If you prepare your puppy's food be sure it receives food rich in protein, such as eggs, beef or chicken. Unless you are prepared to become an expert on canine nutrition, formulating your own dog food is not a good idea, especially for young dogs. Improper balances of minerals, proteins, calories, vitamins and trace elements will result in developmental diseases and unhealthy puppies.

It is a good idea to feed your puppy the same food on the same schedule used by the breeder. Ideally, puppies of seven weeks should be fed three times a day. When they reach five months, the number of feedings can be reduced to twice a day. Because this is a period of rapid growth, be sure to feed your puppy enough. Your veterinarian can tell you how much to feed your puppy.

Keeping Your Puppy Healthy

A proper diet contributes to your puppy's health, but diet is only one aspect of preventive medicine. Immediately after you bring your puppy home, you should take it to the veterinarian for its first examination and vaccinations against a number of infectious diseases. During the first weeks of its life a puppy is protected from disease because it receives passive immunity from its mother (providing she has been properly immunized) while it is nursing. At about six weeks, this passive immunity wears off, and your puppy should start to receive a series of inoculations against distemper, canine hepatitis, leptospirosis, parvovirus and perhaps others. These shots are administered every two to four weeks until the puppy reaches four months. At this time, the puppy should be inoculated against rabies. Some veterinarians also recommend a vaccination against kennel cough. Thereafter, your dog should receive annual booster shots, although some rabies vaccinations are given every three years.

Distemper and rabies are extremely dangerous diseases. Rabies is always fatal, and distemper usually is in young puppies. In older dogs, distemper often causes nerve damage. Vaccinations against these diseases are the only way to protect your dog.

Worms and Worming

Many puppies have worms, especially roundworms which are passed from the mother to the puppy. Although not a serious problem for adult dogs, roundworms can be fatal to a puppy. They also may be involved with human health problems, especially in young children. Symptoms of roundworms include irregular appetite, diarrhea, weakness, cramps and a bloated belly. Roundworms are treated with medication from your veterinarian.

Puppies are also prone to tapeworms, which are often transmitted by fleas; therefore part of the treatment includes getting rid of fleas to ensure that the puppy is not reinfected. Segments of the tapeworm are passed through your dog's stool and are visible to the eye. As the segments, which resemble rice, pass through the dog's intestine they create an uncomfortable feeling, sometimes causing the dog to scoot its rump across the ground. Your veterinarian will administer a shot to treat tapeworms.

Worms and other parasites are discussed in greater detail in FIGHTING YOUR DOG'S PARASITES.

At top: Taking it easy under the sun. *Facing page, above:* A happy, healthy dog and his young owner. *Facing page, below:* A friendly game of tug-of-war. After the initial get-acquainted period, most dogs accept a new puppy in the house.

Teething

Puppies, like humans, are born toothless. At about three to five weeks of age, the puppy's first set of milk teeth appear. Around four months, the permanent teeth will start to come in. The gums may appear swollen as the permanent teeth press on the roots of the temporary teeth. Many puppies chew on hard objects, which encourages the temporary teeth to fall out. Make sure your puppy has many chew toys, so it won't resort to chewing on your shoes or furniture. All of the permanent teeth should be in around eight months of age.

Sometimes the temporary tooth doesn't come out as it should, and is still in place as the permanent tooth comes in. In this case, your vet may need to extract the temporary tooth. This problem is more common in toy breeds.

Getting Acquainted With Other Pets

Many animals may resent a new puppy in the house, so use caution when introducing the newest member of the household. A playful puppy can be irritating to the older dog, who may snap at the puppy. Even a well-meaning adult dog could harm a puppy through rough-housing.

Cats in particular resent the intrusion of a new puppy. In general, they will stay clear of the puppy until they are used to the idea of a new family member. Many a cat has been known to swat a rambunctious puppy, so it is a good idea to trim kitty's front claws. In time, however, cat and dog can live peacefully, if not happily, together.

THE PICTORIAL GUIDE TO DOG CARE

Feeding Your Dog

Like their owners, dogs require a well-balanced diet to keep them feeling healthy and active. The condition of a dog's coat and its level of physical activity are good indicators of a proper diet. A healthy dog has a smooth, shiny coat. Improperly fed dogs have a dull coat and are listless and fatigued.

Most dogs enjoy table scraps, but a diet consisting solely of table scraps may not give your dog the nutrients it needs. If you decide to prepare your dog's food yourself, be sure its diet is nutritionally balanced. Commercial dog foods can provide your dog with all the essential nutrients, and they offer the added benefit of convenience. Commercial dog foods are available in three forms: dry, semimoist and canned. Through a combination of ingredients from both plant and animal sources, these foods are formulated to meet your dog's daily requirements. However, be sure to check that the product is labeled 'Nutritionally complete and balanced.' A product labeled 'All Meat' will need to be supplemented. A healthy diet, whether from the owner's table or from a can or bag, should consist of proteins, fat, carbohydrates, vitamins, minerals, trace elements and water.

Depending on your dog's age and level of activity, 15 to 30 percent of its diet should consist of protein. Protein supplies amino acids, which are necessary for the growth, repair and maintenance of healthy muscles, bones and internal organs. Beef and chicken are good sources of protein, as are bone meal and soybean meal found in commercial dog foods.

Fat is a concentrated source of energy. One gram of fat contains more than twice the calories as one gram of protein or carbohydrates. Fat helps a dog use fat-soluble vitamins (A, D, E and K), and it keeps the skin and coat healthy. Fat deficiency can result in a coarse, dry coat and skin lesions. As we humans know, fat also makes food taste better.

Carbohydrates—starches and sugars—provide your dog with calories and therefore energy. If a dog's diet lacks carbohydrates, its body will convert proteins normally used for growth into needed sugars. Carbohydrates also supply fiber and roughage. Fiber helps prevent diarrhea, constipation and other intestinal problems. Roughage helps clean the digestive tract so that the dog can more efficiently break down its food. Carbohydrates are found in rice, corn, potatoes, oats, wheat and cereals and in the grain, vegetable and starch components of commercial dog food.

Vitamins help the body perform its vital functions, such as growth and fertility. Dogs manufacture some vitamins, such as vitamin C and niacin, but most vitamins come from the food your dog eats. Good sources of vitamins are

Facing page: **The Siberian Husky is so gentle and friendly around people that it does not make a good guard dog.**

brewer's yeast, fresh greens, carrots and fruits. Most commercial foods supply your dog with all the vitamins and minerals it needs, but a home made diet may require supplements. Take care not to over-supplement—an excess of vitamins can be as harmful as a deficiency. Some vitamins can accumulate in toxic amounts. Vitamins A, D, E and K are fat soluble, meaning that the excess is stored rather than excreted.

Minerals also help to regulate bodily functions. Calcium and phosphorous are needed to develop strong teeth and bones in puppies and young dogs. As with vitamins, a mineral supplement is usually not necessary, unless recommended by your veterinarian. Veterinarians see more problems due to oversupplementation than from vitamin and mineral deficiencies.

Trace elements include cobalt, copper, iodine, iron, manganese, selenium and zinc. As the name suggests, these elements are needed in very small amounts and enough can be found in most foods to meet the requirements of your dog.

Water is an essential component of your dog's diet and should not be overlooked. Water is vital to all living cells. It carries nutrients throughout your dog's system and aids in the elimination of waste. A dog's body cannot store much water and an inadequate supply can case severe problems, so be sure to give your dog a fresh supply of water every day. Water is also found in your dog's food. Canned foods are about 75 percent water, while dry foods are about 10 percent.

How Much Food Does My Dog Need?

How much to feed your dog depends on a variety of factors—age, size, activity, temperament, sex, weather. For example, a Golden Retriever used for hunting requires food that provides more energy and more of it than does a less active Golden. A small dog weighing only five pounds needs only 250 calories a day, while a dog of 100 pounds needs about 2300 calories. A dog kept outside in cold weather may need more than 50 percent more calories than it would if kept indoors. A good way to determine if your dog is being fed the proper amount is to weigh it every few weeks. If it is gaining weight, you should cut back on the amount of food and fat intake as well as increase its level of exercise.

Controlling Your Dog's Weight

Dogs gain weight for the same reasons that people do—too much food and not enough exercise. Older dogs are particularly prone to obesity because their owners don't cut back on the amount of food even though the dogs aren't as active as they once were. Overweight dogs are subject to the same health risks as overweight humans—heart and lung diseases; gastrointestinal upsets; bone, joint and muscles problems; and metabolic disorders. In addition, obesity can

Above: Unlike their owners, dogs do not need to eat plenty of fresh fruit and vegetables to stay healthy. *Below:* An assortment of feeding dishes. Note the high sides on the hound dish to keep their long ears out of their dinner.

Proper feeding is as important for the household pet, like this Papillon *(facing page, above)*, as it is for the career Air Force dog *(facing page, below)*.

THE PICTORIAL GUIDE TO DOG CARE

Above: Hunting dogs are extremely loyal and intelligent animals. *Above, right:* Dusty as a puppy and as a grown dog *(right)*. She gained too much weight because the children always shared their food with her. (Notice she has her eye on the candy!) *Facing page:* A boy and his Bearded Collie. Beardies are accustomed to hard work and need regular exercise. Active dogs require more food than less active dogs.

reduce a dog's life expectancy and increase the risks involved with anesthetics and surgery. If you can't easily feel your dog's ribs, it is overweight.

Diet and exercise are the keys to helping your dog back to a healthy weight. To reduce your dog's caloric intake, gradually cut back on its food, or feed it a reduced-calorie commercial food especially formulated for obese dogs. Two or three small meals a day instead of the usual one or two may help to ease your dog's hunger. Be sure to feed your dog only at mealtimes—don't give into begging!

Exercise will also help the reducing process by burning calories rather than storing them as fat. In addition, exercise will strengthen the dog's heart and lungs. Walking is probably the best form of exercise for the overweight dog, but slow down or stop if the dog becomes fatigued. A vigorous game of fetch is too strenuous for the overweight dog and should wait until it is back in shape.

Feeding Time

Most adult dogs are content with one meal a day, usually in the evening. The smaller breeds, however, prefer to eat twice a day. Because dogs like routine, they should have a regular feeding time and place. The kitchen is a logical place because the area can be easily cleaned.

Choosing a feeding bowl is largely a matter of personal preference and price. Plastic bowls are the cheapest, but many a plastic bowl has ended up in pieces all over the kitchen floor. If not completely destroyed, the chew marks make cleaning difficult. Stainless steel bowls are easy to clean—and just as easy to knock over. An earthenware or ceramic bowl offers the advantages of being durable and easy to clean. Dogs with long, floppy ears, such as spaniels and setters, sometimes trail their ears in their food, which can cause dermatitis on the ears. To prevent this, there are deep, narrow bowls that keep their ears out of the food.

THE PICTORIAL GUIDE TO DOG CARE

Your Dog's Health

A healthy dog is alert and interested in its environment. It carries itself proudly—its head held high, its ears attuned to the sounds around it. A healthy dog's coat gleams. Its nose is moist, and both eyes and nose should be free from discharge. Your dog's health is your responsibility. It is up to you to feed it a well-balanced diet, make sure it gets enough exercise, groom it regularly and vaccinate it against the major infectious diseases.

At times, however, your dog is bound to get sick. Your dog cannot tell when it feels sick, so you must learn to read the signs of ill health. Look for changes in its appearance or behavior—it will lose interest in its surroundings, it becomes more introverted and less active. Watch for a change in appetite—both an increase and a decrease in appetite can signal illness. Other signs of illness are:

- thirst
- exhaustion
- poor coat condition
- excessive coughing or sneezing
- frequent wheezing or a runny nose
- repeated vomiting
- pale gums
- bad breath
- slight paralysis or limping
- trembling or shaking
- swelling or lumps on the body
- troubled breathing
- bleeding
- cloudy or orange-colored urine
- inability or uncontrollable urge to urinate
- diarrhea that lasts longer than 24 hours
- moaning or whimpering
- a sticky discharge from the eyes
- unusual slobbering or salivation
- scratching

If you notice any of these signs, contact your veterinarian. A combination of any of these signs may warrant immediate medical attention. It must be stresed that you cannot know the abnormal unless you know the normal. Therefore, you must learn to examine and handle your dog regularly, every day. In addition to recognizing the signs of illness, it is useful to know how to take your dog's temperature and pulse.

Facing page: The highly intelligent German Shepherd requires plenty of exercise and regular brushing to keep it fit and healthy.

A veterinarian checks a Shetland Sheepdog's heart (above) and then reassures her somewhat apprehensive patient (facing page). You should take your dog to the vet every year for annual shots and an examination.

A dog's normal temperature is 100.4 to 102.2 degrees Fahrenheit. The temperature is slightly higher in younger dogs and slightly lower in older dogs. To take a dog's temperature, you will need a rectal thermometer, petroleum jelly to lubricate the thermometer, and, if possible, a friend to hold the dog. Shake the thermometer down to below 99 degrees Fahrenheit. Lubricate the thermometer with the petroleum jelly. Lift the dog's tail and slip the thermometer about one inch into the rectum. Hold it in place for about two minutes. Wash the thermometer in cold water when you are finished.

To take your dog's pulse, place the ball of two fingers over an artery—on the front paw or on the inside of the thigh. You can also feel the pulse over the heart area—low on the left-hand side of the chest (just behind the elbow of a standing dog). Use a watch with a second hand and count the number of beats per 30 seconds or one minute. The pulse for small dogs is 90 to 120 beats per minute; for large dogs the pulse is 65 to 90 beats per minute. Younger dogs have a quicker pulse.

This chapter is arranged according to the ailments that strike the various systems of the body. Its purpose is to help you understand when you need to consult your veterinarian.

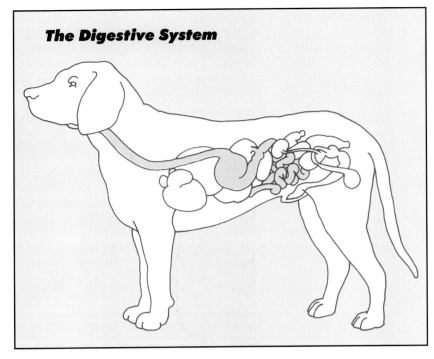

The Digestive System

At top: The digestive system. The long tube is the esophagus, which leads (from left to right) into the stomach, the duodenum and the small intestine. Persistent vomiting and diarrhea are indicative of problems in the digestive tract.

Above: A yellow Labrador Retriever. *Right:* A Great Pyrenees, also known as a Pyrenean Mountain Dog. *Facing page:* Dogs enjoy spending time with their owners, especially for a picnic in the park.

Digestive Disorders

VOMITING. All dogs vomit, and vomiting does not necessarily indicate a medical problem. A dog with newborn puppies, for example, may instinctively regurgitate her food to feed her puppies. Young puppies may overeat, which triggers a vomiting reflex, and nervous dogs may vomit when upset.

If your dog shows no other signs of illness, treat vomiting by not feeding your dog for 24 hours (12 hours for puppies). Water should be available, but only in small quantities, usually less than 1/2 cup at a time. Begin feeding your dog with small, easily digested meals, such as low fat cottage cheese or rice. Feed three tiny meals rather than one big meal. The next day return to the dog's normal food in reduced quantities.

Vomiting is only a problem if it persists. It can be caused by worms, an infection, liver or kidney failure, or an object in any part of the digestive tract. Persistent vomiting may be accompanied by diarrhea. If the vomiting is violent, persists despite the restrictions in food and water intake, or lasts more than 24 hours, the dog must be seen by a veterinarian.

DIARRHEA. Diarrhea, like vomiting, is a sign of numerous canine disorders, from worms to poisoning to intestinal blockages, but, in general, the occasional bout of diarrhea is not a cause for concern. If your dog is otherwise healthy, diarrhea may be a sign of a minor intestinal upset. To treat simple diarrhea, feed your dog starches such as rice and macaroni. If the problem persists or is accompanied by other signs of illness, consult a veterinarian. Diarrhea can lead to dehydration and depression if left untreated. If blood is present in the stools, contact your vet immediately.

CONSTIPATION. Constipation is common in older dogs and in dogs that eat bones. Early signs include very hard stools and straining to pass a stool. It can usually be treated by changing your dog's diet and including a bulk, fiber type product, such as unprocessed bran or 'psylliun seed' laxative available in the pharmacy. Never use a chemical laxative or any human medicines without strict veterinary instructions. Constipation may also be the result of your dog swallowing a hard object. If you suspect that your dog has swallowed a foreign object, do not administer a laxative. The object will have to be removed surgically.

Contact your vet if the problem continues for more than two days, if your dog is unable to pass a stool, or if constipation recurs. Recurring constipation may be a sign of another problem, such as a rectal tumor or an enlarged prostate.

ENTERITIS. An infection or inflammation of the intestinal tract, regardless of the cause, is called enteritis. The cause may be bacteria, poisons, worms or swallowing sharp objects. Often accompanied by diarrhea, this condition can be very uncomfortable for your dog. Enteritis is often the signal for a more serious illness, such as parvovirus, so contact your vet if your dog exhibits these symptoms.

BLOCKED ANAL DUCTS. If you notice your dog scooting its rump along the ground, its anal ducts may be blocked. Your vet will empty the anal sacs by squeezing them to force out the contents of the sacs. This ailment is more common among smaller breeds than larger ones.

TONSILLITIS. Tonsillitis is usually caused by an oral infection. Sometimes plant seeds and weeds will lodge in the tonsillar crypts. Symptoms include fever, lack of appetite and coughing and gagging. Tonsillitis is usually treated with antibiotics; surgery is almost never necessary.

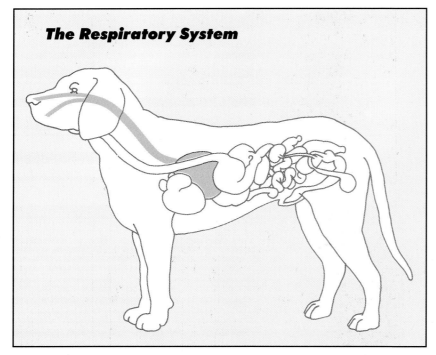

The Respiratory System

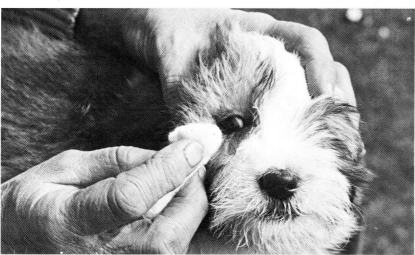

At top: The respiratory system, showing the dog's airways (pharynx, larynx, trachea and bronchi) and lungs. *Above:* A discharge is the most common sign of eye disease. To remove the discharge, gently wipe the area around the eye with a piece of gauze soaked in warm water or a commercial eye wash. *Facing page:* A vet treats an eye disorder.

Respiratory Disorders

COUGHING. Coughing is a sign of many canine diseases and indicates an inflammation in the dog's airway. If no other signs of illness are present, coughing may be the result of too much barking or smoke/dust irritation and should clear up within 48 hours. However, coughing can also signal a foreign object in the throat, a chronic infection such as bronchitis or laryngitis, kennel cough, heart disease or distemper. A harsh, dry cough like whooping cough suggests kennel cough, while a soft cough may indicate a lung problem.

DISEASES OF THE AIRWAYS. Like humans, dogs are subject to laryngitis, bronchitis and emphysema. In both laryngitis and bronchitis, the walls of the airway are thickened, making the airway smaller. As the disease progresses, the wall may swell permanently. The end result is chronic coughing and decreased tolerance for exercise.

Emphysema is a similar disease affecting the lungs. It, too, impairs a dog's ability to exercise. Emphysema is not as common in dogs as it is in people, perhaps because dogs are too smart to smoke cigarets! All of these conditions are treated with medication to reduce inflammation and expand the airways. Antibiotics are frequently used to combat secondary infections.

PNEUMONIA. A rough cough, shallow breathing, nasal discharge, loss of appetite and high fever are symptoms of pneumonia. Once a fatal disease, and still potentially life threatening, pneumonia is now often successfully treated with antibiotics and other drugs.

SOFT PALATE PROBLEMS. Short-nosed dogs (Pugs, Pekinese and Bull-dogs) are prone to respiratory problems resulting from a congenital defect of the soft palate. The soft palate may be too long and lie in the opening to the larynx, causing snorting, noisy breathing and eventually, chronic inflammation and laryngitis. In severe cases, surgery may be the necessary, although it may not completely correct the problem.

Eye Disorders

Most eye disorders require the attention of a veterinarian, in some cases immediately. In the meantime, irrigating the eye can ease the discomfort until the vet can see your dog. To irrigate the eye, hold the eye open with your thumb and finger. Rinse the eye with a gentle stream of sterile, ophthalmic eye wash or human contact lens lubricating solution from the pharmacy.

DISCHARGE FROM THE EYE. A discharge from the eye is the most common sign of eye disease. A clear discharge can be caused by an irritation or inflammation, such as conjunctivitis. It can also signal blocked tear ducts. A cloudy discharge, one that is thick and discolored, is generally an indication of infection and requires the immediate attention of a veterinarian.

SWOLLEN EYE. A protruding eyeball results when the tissues behind the eye swell, pushing the eye forward. This is a serious condition, having several possible causes: a blow to the head, a car accident, an infection behind the eye, a tumor, glaucoma. Other danger signs include a glazed stare, dilated pupil and lids unable to close. Your dog is in danger of losing its eye—consult a vet immediately.

CONJUNCTIVITIS. 'Pink eye' is the common term for conjunctivitis. In this condition, the mucous membranes that line the inner surface of the eyelids and the forepart of the eyeball become inflamed. Conjunctivitis can be caused by an infection, a scratch, a congenital disorder, a tumor on the lid, or an irritant such as dust or smoke. Signs include tears, redness and screwing up the eye.

KERATITIS. When the cornea is inflamed it becomes cloudy or even powder blue and completely opaque. This condition is called 'blue eye' and is seen in dogs with hepatitis. Corneal ulcers and irritations also cause local areas to become white or bluish. The eye in such cases is usually extremely painful, and will be kept partially or tightly shut. Such a condition warrants immediate veterinary medical attention. Other color changes can signify ongoing problems with the cornea. The white of the eye may become severely congested, and then chronic inflammation can lead to a film of black pigment across the eye. If the cause of the inflammation is treated soon enough, the condition *may* be halted. As a last resort, the black film can also be removed through surgery.

CATARACTS. Cataracts are opaque areas in the lens of the eye which impair a dog's vision. The condition can be inherited, or may develop as a complication of other diseases such as diabetes. Older dogs often develop clouding of the

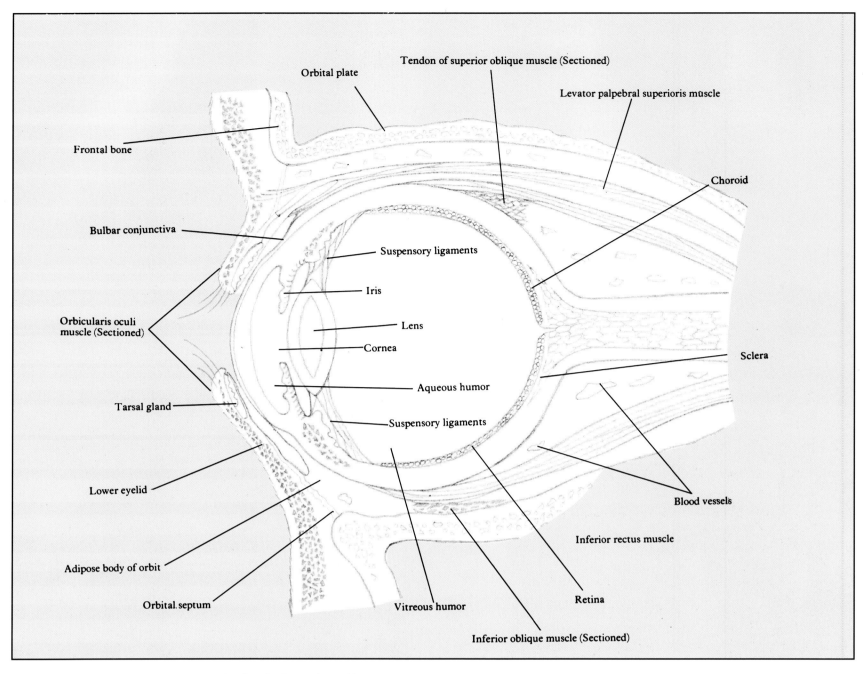

Orbital plate

Tendon of superior oblique muscle (Sectioned)

Levator palpebral superioris muscle

Frontal bone

Choroid

Bulbar conjunctiva

Suspensory ligaments

Iris

Orbicularis oculi
muscle (Sectioned)

Lens

Cornea

Sclera

Aqueous humor

Tarsal gland

Suspensory ligaments

Lower eyelid

Blood vessels

Inferior rectus muscle

Adipose body of orbit

Orbital septum

Vitreous humor

Retina

Inferior oblique muscle (Sectioned)

Above: **A cross section of the eye. Shetland Sheepdogs *(facing page, above)* are prone to central PRA. Dachshunds *(facing page, below)*, among other breeds, are affected by generalized PRA.**

lenses, but since many dogs manage to cope with the condition, it isn't always necessary to treat it. In severe cases, specialist eye surgeons can remove the diseased lens, preventing blindness.

GLAUCOMA. This disease involves the drainage system of the inside of the eye. The eye produces fluids to nourish it. Sometimes the fluids build up when the drainage outlets become blocked. As a result, the globe stretches and the eye becomes severely inflamed. The pain makes the dog shed tears continually. Glaucoma should be treated by a veterinarian immediately, as the condition, if left untreated, may progress to blindness within a matter of hours. Treatment may be surgical or rely on drugs to reduce fluid production, constrict the pupil and improve internal drainage.

CONGENITAL DEFECTS OF THE EYELID AND EYELASHES. Unfortunately, dogs' eyes are prone to a number of congenital defects. Common defects of the eyelids are entropion and ectropion. In entropion, the eyelid turns inward, causing the lashes to dig into the surface of the eye. In ectropion, the opposite occurs—the eyelid turns outward, causing tears to pool in the pouch formed by the lid. This can lead to chronic inflammation and conjunctivitis.

Trichiasis, a defect of the eyelashes, refers to any condition that brings the eyelashes into direct contact with the eye. Trichiasis causes frequent squinting, excessive tearing, conjunctivitis and can lead to corneal ulceration. Distichiasis is a similar problem where extra hairs on the lid rub on the eye, causing pain and redness. This condition can be alleviated by removing the hairs surgically or through electrolysis.

DISORDERS OF THE RETINA. Progressive retinal atrophy (PRA) is a hereditary disease that progresses for months or even years. In this disease, the blood supply to the retina withers away and the light-sensitive cells die. This disorder takes two forms—central PRA and generalized PRA. The central form may not cause total blindness, but the generalized one often does. Golden

Retrievers, Labradors, Collies and Shetland Sheepdogs are prone to central PRA, while Cairn Terriers, Cocker Spaniels, Dachshunds, Poodles and Irish Setters are prone to generalized PRA.

Collie eye anomaly (CEA) is present in a distressingly high number of Collies and Shetland Sheepdogs. This disorder can lead to retinal hemorrhage or a detached retina, both of which can cause blindness.

PROBLEMS OF THE THIRD EYELID. Dogs have a third eyelid on each eye, known as the haw, or nictating membrane. The third eyelid is mainly hidden under the lower lid, with just a small part of the pigmented edge visible in the corner of the eye close to the nose. This lid acts as a windshield wiper for the eye, sweeping away foreign objects, as well as providing about 15 percent of the tear secretion.

In some breeds, such as the St Bernard and the Bloodhound, the third eyelid is prominent, but in most dogs a protruding third eyelid indicates illness or disease. Problems of the third eyelid can be caused by a painful eye condition, weight loss, scrolled cartilage (a congenital deformity) and prolapsed nictitans gland. Signs to watch for include a whitish membrane, usually with a black edge protruding from the inner corner of the eye and a reddish, pea-shaped lump in the inner corner of the eye.

BLINDNESS. Blindness results from a number of causes, but in many cases it can be difficult to detect because dogs learn how to compensate for their lack of sight. A dog's excellent sense of hearing, combined with its knowledge of its surroundings, gives it a remarkable ability to cope. However, a blind dog removed from its own environment will be more tentative. If you take your blind dog for a walk, it will probably stay close at hand. It is essential to keep it on a leash to protect it from the dangers of automobile traffic and the neighborhood swimming pool or pond. You can ease its discomfort by speaking to it frequently. At home, do not rearrange the furniture, and if you leave the dog alone in the house, the sound of the radio will lessen its sense of isolation.

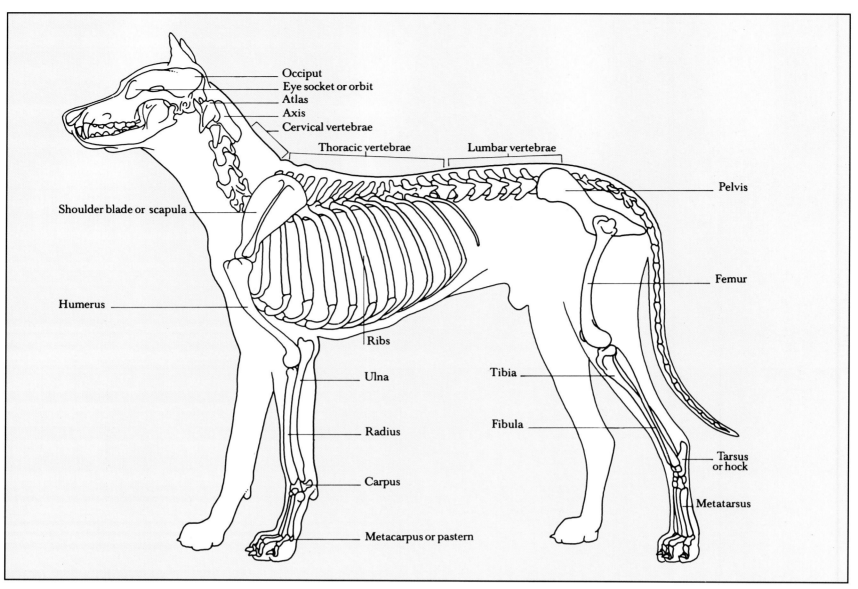

Labels on skeleton diagram:
Occiput
Eye socket or orbit
Atlas
Axis
Cervical vertebrae
Thoracic vertebrae
Lumbar vertebrae
Pelvis
Shoulder blade or scapula
Femur
Humerus
Ribs
Ulna
Tibia
Radius
Fibula
Carpus
Tarsus or hock
Metatarsus
Metacarpus or pastern

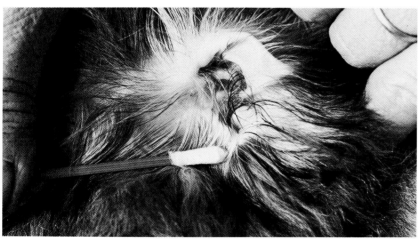

At top: **The dog's skeleton has two major types of bones — long bones (the tubular bones like the leg bones and the spine) and flat bones (such as the skull and pelvis). The basic design of the dog has remained unchanged since the early days of its evolution; however, there has been considerable modification in the limbs of the various breeds. Compare the structure of a Basset Hound to that of a Greyhound.** *Above:* **When you groom your dog, you should check its ears for signs of infection, such as a discharge. Clean the ear gently with a Q-tip,** *never* **probing where you cannot see.** *Facing page:* **An ear exam by a vet.**

Ear Disorders

DISCHARGE FROM THE EARS. A discharge from the ears is a symptom of an outer ear infection. A dark, gritty discharge is typical with ear mites; a runny, black or a thick, yellow discharge accompanied by a foul odor could be a yeast or bacterial infection. All of these conditions are treated with the appropriate medication, as prescribed by your veterinarian.

SWOLLEN EAR FLAP. If your dog shakes its head, paws at its ear, or tilts its head, it may have a swollen ear flap. A soft, fluid swelling on the inside of the ear flap is often an aural hematoma (a blood blister). This condition can be caused by a blow to the ear, an ear infection that causes the dog to shake its head, or a dog fight. Surgery is typically the treatment for a swollen ear.

LOSS OF HEARING. Deafness in young dogs is unusual, but some infections may temporarily impair hearing. If your dog does not respond when you call it, and also exhibits symptoms of ear problems (pain, tilting the head, scratching, discharge), it may be suffering from a loss of hearing. Possible causes include inner ear infection, wax blocking the ear canal, or chronic disease blocking the outer ear. Deafness can also be caused by a congenital defect or a genetic cause. Check the ear for any wax or hair that may be blocking the ear canal. If you suspect an infection, take your dog to the vet as soon as possible.

Bone and Joint Disorders

HIP DYSPLASIA. Hip dysplasia is a disease common to large breeds of dogs, particularly German Shepherds, Labrador Retrievers and Golden Retrievers. It is a malformation of the hip joint, resulting in an improper fit of the ball end of the thigh and the socket of the hip. Hip dysplasia is a serious and painful disorder, leading to permanent physical damage, including lameness and loss of the use of the back legs. Treatment ranges from painkillers to surgery. Surgery involves altering the shape of the hip socket to create a better fit, or completely replacing the hip. The latter procedure, while very successful, can only be performed by a limited number of specialists.

The problem cannot usually be detected in a young puppy. Signs of the disorder do not show up until at least five months of age, but the best time for

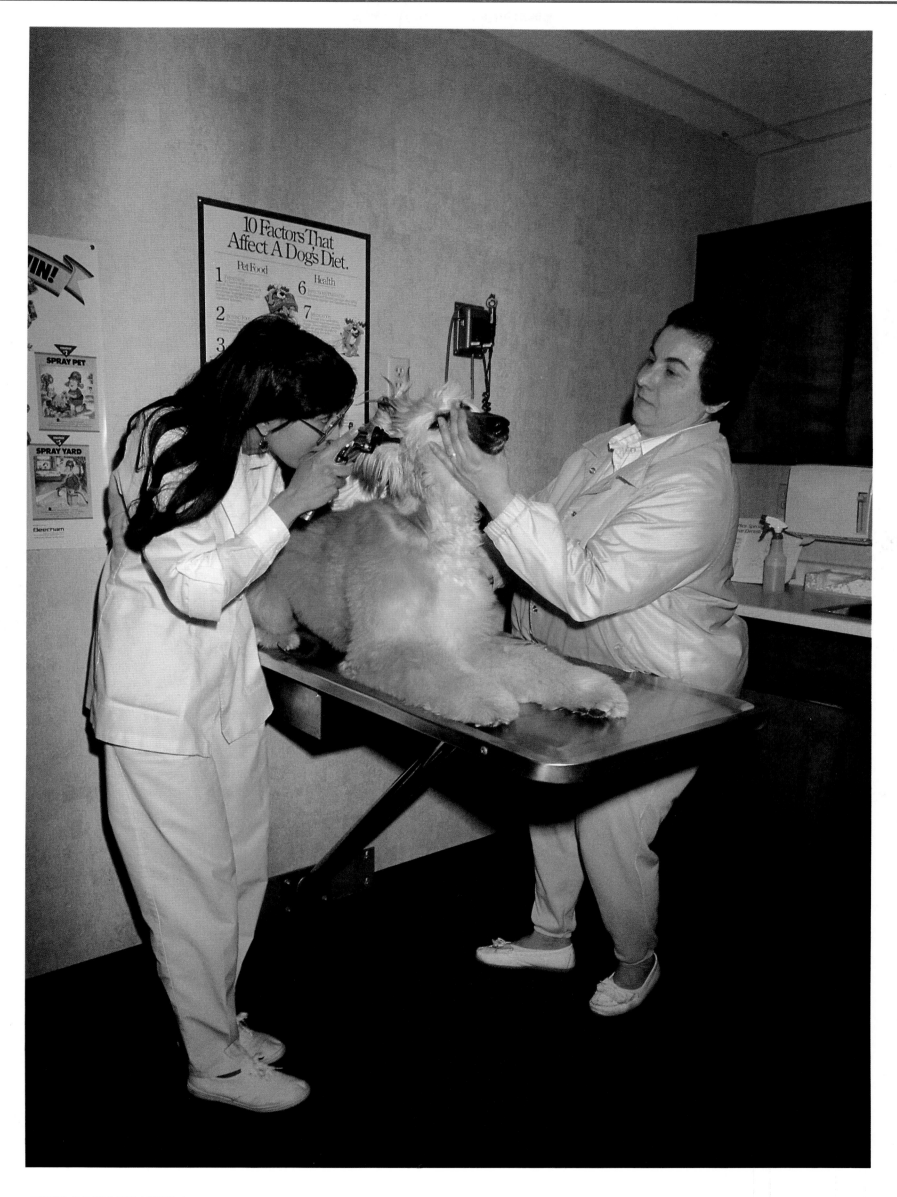

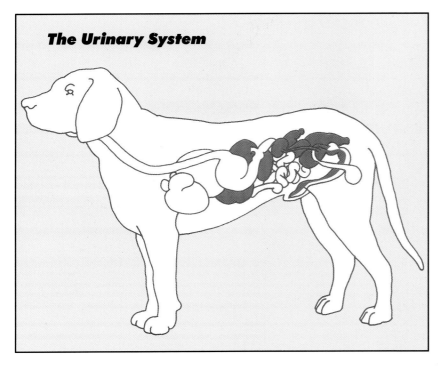

The Urinary System

At top: The urinary system, showing the kidneys (the small, bean-shaped organ). The narrow tube, leading to the bladder, is the ureter. The large organ on the left is the liver, which is part of the upper digestive tract. Both the liver and the kidneys rid the body of toxins. *Above:* Prescription diets are available for dogs with specific health problems, such as kidney disease or obesity.

A number of large breeds—such as Golden Retrievers *(facing page, above)* and Irish Setters *(facing page, below)*—are prone to hip dysplasia, an inherited disease affecting the hip joint. The condition is diagnosed by X-ray.

diagnosis is between two and three years of age. Hip dysplasia is quite often an inherited condition, so many medical and breed societies have established a certification process to ensure that bloodlines are free of the disorder. In the United States, the Orthopedic Foundation of America (OFA) certification guarantees that a dog has been X-rayed and is free of hip dysplasia. When purchasing a pedigreed puppy of a breed prone to this disorder, ask to see the OFA certification for the parents.

ARTHRITIS. Like people, dogs are prone to arthritis, an inflammation of the joints. Its may be hereditary, caused by nutritional deficiencies, injuries, infection or systemic disease. Limping is one of the first signs of arthritis.

OSTEOARTHRITIS. Osteoarthritis is an inflammation of the bone on the joint. There is frequently no cure, so treatment is usually aimed at reducing the inflammation and alleviating the pain. Rest is extremely important. The drawback to pain killers is that they enable the dog to use the injured joint when it should be resting it.

OSTEOCHONDRITIS DISSECANS. This a fairly common problem seen especially in large breeds. As a result of faulty circulatory nourishment to the joint surface, an area of shoulder cartilage dies and falls into the joint, where it sometimes forms a loose lump called a 'joint mouse.' The lump rubs on the joint and can cause arthritis. Surgery to remove the joint mouse usually results in a complete recovery. The elbow, knee and hock bones can also be affected. This disease is most likely the result of over-rapid development.

OSTEOPOROSIS. Osteoporosis is a nutritional bone disease caused by, among other things, an imbalanced calcium-phosphorous ration in the diet. An all-meat diet, for example, is too high in phosphorous. Although the bones appear normal, they are weak and break easily. A proper diet is the best way to prevent this disease from occurring, but treatment may consist of vitamins or a special diet.

RICKETS. True rickets is the result of a deficiency of vitamin D. The dog cannot use calcium properly, and the bones become weak and bend, while the joints enlarge. Rickets-like diseases are found in puppies that grow rapidly without receiving a nutritionally balanced diet.

Liver Disorders

CHRONIC LIVER DISEASE. This long-term condition is often difficult to diagnose. Signs include weight loss, with or without a poor appetite; dullness; increased thirst; vomiting; diarrhea and/or pale feces; distended abdomen; stupidity; and seizures. Chronic liver disease may follow several bouts of acute (sudden and severe) liver disease. On the other hand, acute liver disease may follow years of chronic liver disease. The long-term prognosis is poor, and may eventually affect the brain.

Treatment concentrates on making your dog comfortable. Diet must be strictly controlled. If the brain is affected, your dog should be on a low protein diet, but even if the brain is not affected the dog should have high carbohydrates and low fat levels, along with easily digested protein such as eggs, cheese and meat. In addition, your vet may recommend steroids and vitamin supplements—B complex and K.

ACUTE LIVER DISEASE. Symptoms of acute liver disease are abdominal pain, lack of appetite, vomiting, high temperature, jaundice, hemorrhages in the gums, pale feces and dark urine. If your dog has a combination of any of these symptoms, you should rush it to the vet. Recovery from acute liver disease, difficult to begin with, is made worse by delay. Treatment includes antibiotics, steroids, vitamins, intravenous fluids and strict dietary control.

Urinary Disorders

ACUTE KIDNEY DISEASE. Kidney disease is a major cause of death in dogs, and therefore requires the immediate attention of a veterinarian. Signs of acute kidney failure are dullness, vomiting, loss of appetite, bad breath, abdominal pain and not passing any urine. Possible causes are poisoning, leptospirosis, paralysis of the bladder and chronic kidney problems. Kidney disease is treated with antibiotics, intravenous fluid therapy, dialysis, vitamins, or anti-emetics.

CHRONIC KIDNEY DISEASE. Symptoms of chronic kidney disease include excessive thirst, frequent urination, mouth ulcers, weight loss, anemia and bad breath. Treatment involves fluid therapy, supportive care and a low protein diet.

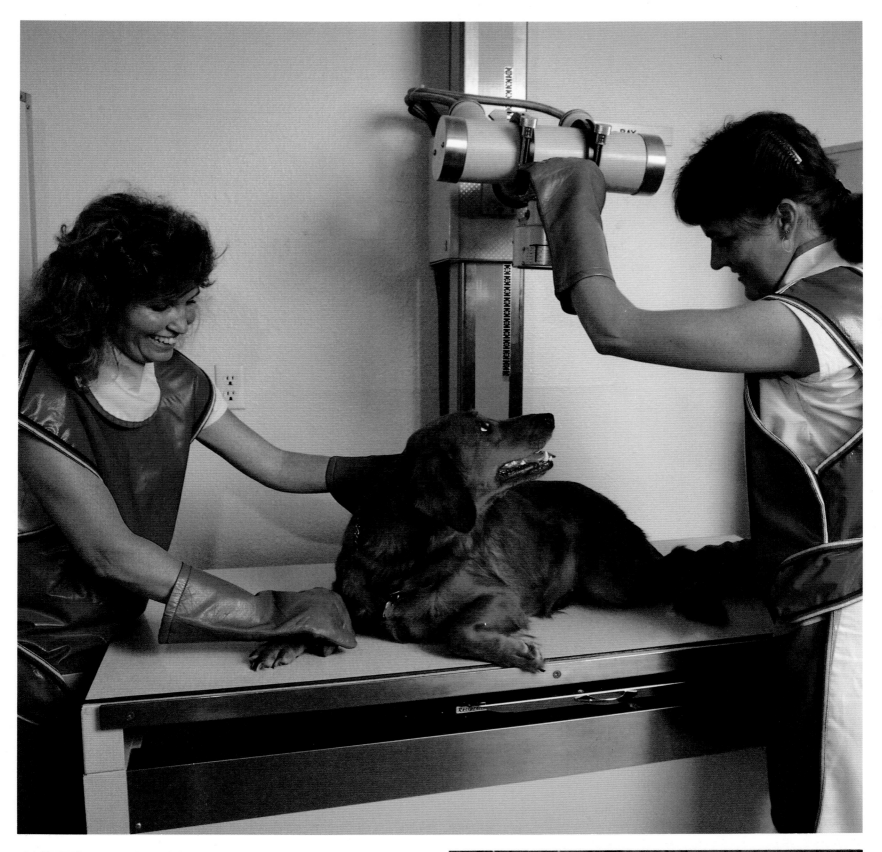

CYSTITIS. Cystitis is an infection or inflammation of the bladder. In mild cases, your dog will be given a urinary acidifier to make the urine less alkaline, which prevents bacteria growth. Signs include frequent urination and blood in the urine. Chronic cystitis often results in the formation of stones in the bladder (see below). This disease is most common in female dogs. Your veterinarian will perform a urinalysis and culture the dog's urine to determine the type of infection and the appropriate antibiotic to use.

STONES IN THE BLADDER. Salts in the urine sometimes form stones, which rub against the bladder causing irritation. The irritation forces your dog to urinate frequently, even though it may pass only a small amount, often with blood in it. In many cases, your dog will strain to pass urine. The stones will need to be removed surgically. Special medications and diets will be used to prevent recurrence.

STONES IN THE URETHRA. In male dogs, stones sometimes form in the urethra, creating a blockage. Urgent treatment—sometimes surgery—is called for, otherwise the pressure will rupture the bladder or damage the kidneys. In addition, the build-up of toxins in your dog's system can be fatal. Signs to watch for are straining to urinate, lack of appetite and vomiting.

The Circulatory System

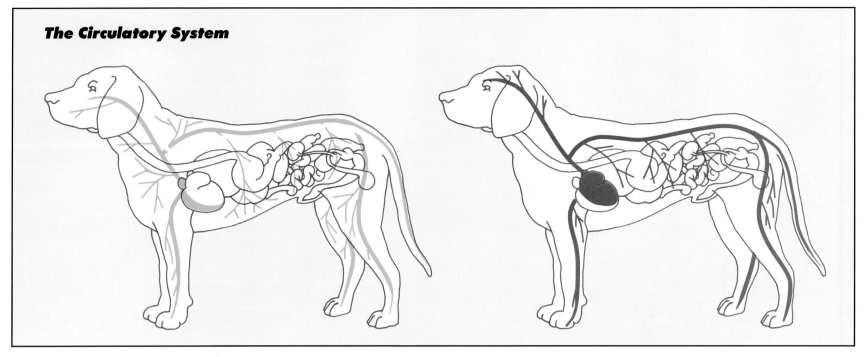

The Heart

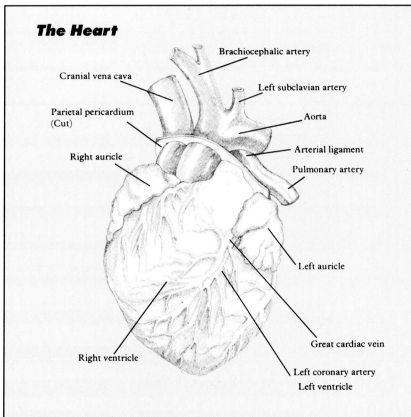

Brachiocephalic artery

Cranial vena cava

Left subclavian artery

Parietal pericardium (Cut)

Aorta

Arterial ligament

Right auricle

Pulmonary artery

Left auricle

Great cardiac vein

Right ventricle

Left coronary artery

Left ventricle

The circulatory system consists of the heart and a network of veins *(top left)* and arteries *(top right)*. The two atria of the heart *(above)* empty blood into the ventricles. The right ventricle pumps blood to the lungs to eliminate carbon dioxide and pick up oxygen. The blood then returns to the left atrium, where it is emptied into the left ventricle to be pumped through the body. *Facing page:* A Cavalier King Charles Spaniel.

Heart and Blood Disorders

ANEMIA. Anemia is a condition in which blood is deficient in the number of red blood cells and/or hemoglobin. Anemia results when 1) red blood cells are destroyed by parasites, poisons, bacterial toxins and immune reactions; 2) blood is lost through an accident, poisoning, bleeding ulcers or parasites, such as whipworms and hookworms; 3) production of red blood cells in the bone marrow is abnormal or reduced due to tumors, poisons, acute infections, chronic kidney disease, mineral deficiencies (iron, copper or cobalt) or vitamin deficiencies (vitamins B6 and B12).

The symptoms of anemia are pallor around the eyes and in the mouth, weakness, inability to exercise, rapid breathing and restlessness. Treatment focuses on the cause of the anemia. In addition, your vet may prescribe iron supplements, vitamins and anabolic steroids. Severe cases may require a blood transfusion. Your dog will need plenty of rest during its recovery period.

HEART MURMUR. A heart murmur is a problem involving the valves of the heart. When the ventricles of the heart contract to pump blood out, the valves should close to prevent the blood from flowing back to the atria of the heart. Sometimes the valves don't close properly and blood leaks back to the atria. This leakage, called a murmur, can be heard through a stethoscope.

Older dogs, especially small breeds, tend to develop heart murmurs. Some puppies have what is known as an 'innocent heart murmur.' Usually the cause is congenital and the condition corrects itself as the puppy grows up.

Many dogs with heart murmers are completely free of symptoms, so it is important to have your veterinarian auscultate, or listen to the dog's heart regularly. A heart murmer can be the first sign of impending cardiac failure. Symptoms of heart failure include tiring easily during exercise and coughing after a period of sleep or rest (known as a cardiac cough). In some forms the abdomen may swell noticeably. These symptoms can often be controlled with medication. In addition, you should monitor your dog's weight closely because obesity places a strain on the heart.

Other Disorders

DIABETES MELLITUS. More commonly seen in female dogs, diabetes mellitus results when the pancreas does not produce enough insulin. Dachshunds, King Charles Spaniels, Poodles and Scottish Terriers are all prone to diabetes.

Insulin helps the cells of the body use the glucose in the blood for energy. In a diabetic dog, the various organs have a hard time metabolizing this glucose and levels in the blood become very high. When glucose levels are high, the glucose is filtered through the kidneys, drawing water with it.

If your dog exhibits heavy thirst, hunger, tiredness and weight loss, it may be diabetic. Take it to the vet for blood and urine tests. Mild cases of diabetes can be controlled through a diet low in carbohydrates and fat and high in fiber. Fiber helps a dog absorb glucose more evenly.

Most cases of diabetes are treated with regular insulin injections, which you can administer at home. You will also need to monitor the amount of glucose in the urine. Diabetes can effectively be kept under control providing you follow a strict schedule for injections and meals. If your dog misses a meal, the injected

The Nervous System

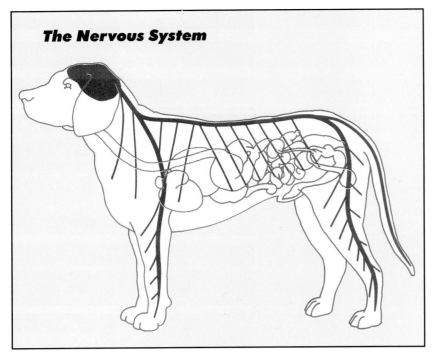

At top: The nervous system—the brain, spine and nerves that radiate to all parts of the body—is the control and communications center of the body. Epilepsy is a disease that affects the nervous system. *Above:* A young boy is delighted with his new playmate. *Right:* A healthy Collie puppy relaxing. *Facing page:* An even-tempered dog assists these students as they study to be animal health technicians.

insulin has no glucose to work on, which could lead to a hypoglycemic coma, collapse and convulsions. Overexertion can also bring on a hypoglycemic coma. As a precaution, have honey or glucose syrup on hand to give orally for emergencies.

EPILEPSY. Epilepsy is fairly common, especially in dogs between one and three years old. It can be caused by an injury, lack of oxygen to the brain, distemper or a tumor. Epilepsy is also an inherited condition. Epilepsy is characterized by seizures. During a seizure, the dog may foam at the mouth, chew, pass urine or feces and paddle its legs. Leave your dog alone during a seizure. Afterwards, let the dog relax. The dog can have water immediately but not much food.

Seizures are generally short, about five minutes, and include a period of unconsciousness. There is no set pattern for seizures. Some dogs have seizures frequently, other dogs less so. Two seizures close together are not necessarily an indication that the epilepsy is getting worse, but any seizure that lasts longer than ten or fifteen minutes may indicate an emergency condition. The seizures may worsen with age, but this could be related to other diseases. Treatment for epilepsy is long-term use of anticonvulsants as prescribed by your veterinarian.

FALSE PREGNANCY. A hormonal imbalance may cause a false pregnancy in your female dog. A false pregnancy often begins up to eight or nine weeks after a heat and may last a few weeks. In itself, a false pregnancy is not dangerous; however, the accompanying behavioral changes can cause problems. Your dog will behave as if she is really pregnant. Her appetite will increase, her abdomen will swell, she will hide away with her imaginary puppies—an old slipper, a stuffed animal—and she may even produce milk.

Usually the condition disappears by itself. If it recurs, your vet will recommend some form of treatment. Some vets prefer hormone therapy, others favor removal of the ovaries. Surgery should not be performed until all symptoms of the false pregnancy have disappeared.

Caring for a Sick Dog

A sick dog, like a sick person, needs extra loving care. Make sure your dog has a warm, comfortable place to sleep. Your dog may have lost its appetite, so you will have to encourage it to eat. A good way to coax your dog to eat is to sit beside it and talk to it reassuringly. Your dog might be more inclined to eat if you feed it out of your hand. If it won't eat its regular food, tempt it with good-tasting nourishing foods. Give it something high in protein that is easily digested such as beef, cheese, eggs, rice, baby cereals or meat-and fish-based baby foods. If all else fails, you may have to resort to spoonfeeding. If your vet has prescribed a special diet, be sure to follow his or her instructions.

It's likely you will have to give your dog medication. Many dogs will swallow a pill if its hidden in a bit of meat or cheese, but check to see that your dog has actually swallowed the pill. Many dogs have learned to hide pills and spit them out when you aren't looking. You can also give your dog a pill by holding it by the upper jaw and lifting its head up. Quickly pop the pill into the back of its mouth and then close its mouth. Tilt the head straight up and rub the throat to encourage swallowing. Liquid medication can be administered with a syringe.

Protecting Your Dog Against Serious Diseases

Preventive medicine is the best way to care for your dog. Vaccination—a vital part of preventive medicine—works by stimulating a dog's immune system to manufacture disease-fighting antibodies. All adult dogs should be vaccinated once a year against the major diseases—canine distemper, infectious canine hepatitis, parvovirus, leptospirosis and rabies. Some rabies vaccines are administered every three years. See CARING FOR YOUR PUPPY for details on immunizing a puppy.

CANINE DISTEMPER. Distemper attacks a dog's respiratory, nervous and digestive systems. It occurs most often in puppies between three and six months old, but can attack dogs of any age. This disease was once the number one killer of puppies, but is now effectively combatted by a vaccination.

Early signs are diarrhea, fever, listlessness and cold symptoms. At a variable interval after the initial infection, the nervous system may be affected. Symptoms range from slight tremors to epileptic fits, blindness and paralysis. Treatment includes antibiotics, cough suppressants, medication for vomiting and diarrhea, and anticonvulsants, but the disease is often fatal. Vaccination to prevent the disease is the real answer.

INFECTIOUS CANINE HEPATITIS. Infectious canine hepatitis, also called Rubarth's disease, is a highly contagious viral disease mostly affecting young dogs. The disease is transmitted though an infected animal's stools, urine or saliva. Symptoms include vomiting, diarrhea, abdominal pain, lack of coordination of the hind legs, convulsions and changes in the appearance of the eye.

Veterinary treatment is essential and may include steroids, antibiotics, transfusions, fluid therapy and kaolin-type preparations.

Facing page: During an exam, the vet checks the skin and coat for lumps and bumps or areas of matted hair suggesting skin punctures.

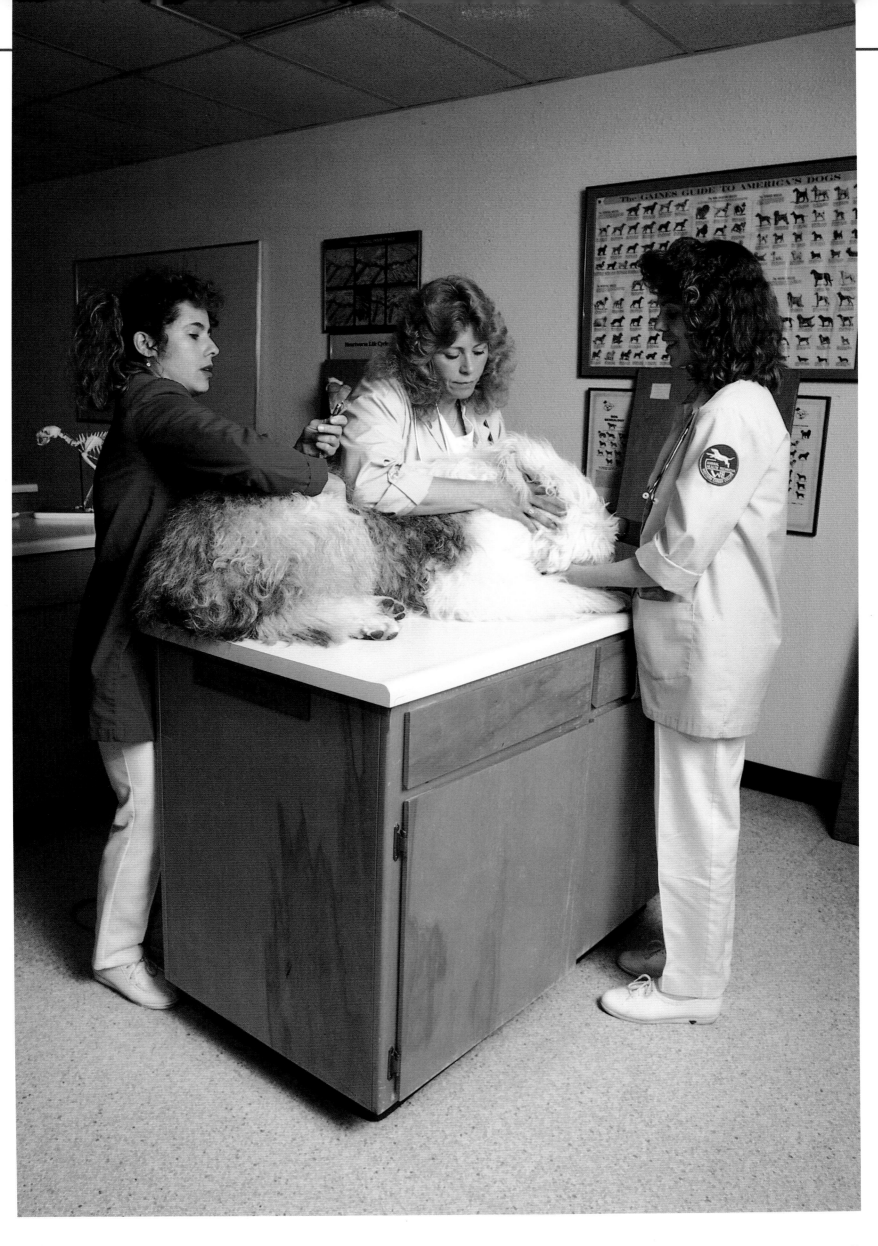

At top: A happy dog joins her owner for a folk song. Above: Grooming is an essential component of health care, especially for long-haired breeds, such as Collies. Facing page: A Cocker Spaniel has its eyes examined. Cockers are prone to generalized PRA (see text, page 58-59).

PARVOVIRUS. Parvovirus is a highly contagious gastrointestinal virus. A relatively new disease (prevalent since only 1978), parvovirus strikes suddenly and can be fatal if not treated promptly. It is transmitted through an infected animal's secretions or stools, and usually strikes unvaccinated puppies. In most cases, the major signs are bloody diarrhea, acute vomiting, listlessness and dehydration.

LEPTOSPIROSIS. There are two forms of leptospirosis—one affects the liver, the other the kidneys. Both are spread through infected urine. Signs include listlessness, loss of appetite, lethargy, vomiting, diarrhea, fever, jaundice, mouth ulcers and extreme weight loss. Treatment includes fluid therapy, drugs to stop vomiting, intestinal sedatives and blood transfusions. If not treated, serious liver and kidney damage, or even death, can result. This is one of the dog diseases that is contageous to people.

RABIES. Rabies is a killer viral disease that is transmitted through the bite of an infected animal. Because it affects the central nervous system, the disease can cause furious running as well as paralysis. Dogs in the highly excitable stage are sensitive to noise and may bite anything that moves. Infected animals always die. A human that has been bitten by an infected animal must be treated with a post-exposure series of vaccinations. All dogs should be vaccinated against rabies. Such vaccination is required by law in most states.

PARAINFLUENZA. Vaccinations are also available for parainfluenza, one of the causes of tracheobronchitis, or kennel cough. Although most cases of kennel cough are caused by a combination of factors, the vaccination offers some protection. Kennel cough is most prevalent during the summer and spreads rapidly among dogs in close quarters, such as kennels and dog shows.

The symptoms of the disease are continual, harsh, dry coughing, loss of appetite, nasal or eye discharge and depression (general lack of interest, lying around). If neglected, the disease can cause serious damage to the respiratory system.

THE PICTORIAL GUIDE TO DOG CARE

Fighting Your Dog's Parasites

Dogs are subject to attack by external and internal parasites. External parasites include fleas, lice, ticks and ringworm. Internal parasites include roundworms, tapeworms, hookworms and whipworms.

External Parasites

FLEAS. Fleas are the bane of dogs and their owners. They are extremely difficult to get rid of, they make your dog uncomfortable by causing skin irritations and they can lead to tapeworms—which cause further problems for your dog.

Although dog fleas are different from cat and human fleas, they are not very discriminating and will feed on you, too. Adult fleas feed on your dog's blood. Their bites will make the dog scratch, and some dogs develop a severe skin irritation from an allergy to flea bites.

Check for fleas if your dog scratches constantly. Fleas tend to congregate near the base of a dog's tail or on its belly. If you don't see any fleas, look for flea dirt—the dark, gritty specks that are actually dried blood and flea feces. You might also notice flea eggs—white specks that look like salt, although typically the eggs fall off and later hatch.

And therein lies the major problem in fighting fleas. The eggs hatch and infest your home. Therefore, you need to treat the environment as well as your dog for fleas. Fleas merely feed on the dog; they live in your house—in your carpets, on the furniture, in the draperies. Dogs that spend a lot of time outside can be continuously reinfested with fleas.

Fleas can be treated with sprays, powders and dips. Flea collars and tags are also available, but are less effective than other treatments, especially on larger dogs. The best approach is to bathe your dog to get rid of the fleas and then use some kind of treatment, such as a dip, that has a residual effect. Using a flea comb on a daily basis will help to prevent the infestation from recurring (or at least keep fleas to a minimum).

Facing page: **Bearded Collies require regular brushing, but all dogs need to be groomed during flea season. Daily grooming controls fleas and alerts the owner to potential problems, such as tumors.**

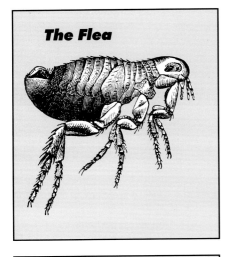

The Flea

The Tick

The Harvest Mite

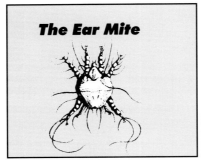

The Ear Mite

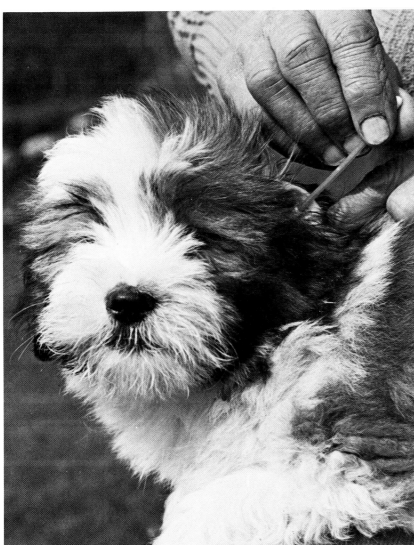

In the meantime, treat your house with a flea bomb or a long-acting environmental spray. In severe cases, a professional exterminator may be necessary. Vacuuming also helps to rid your house of fleas, but be sure to dispose of the vacuum bags so the fleas (or their eggs) don't reinfest your home.

TICKS. Ticks are bloodsuckers. They attach themselves to a dog's skin with its mouth, feed on its blood for a few days and then fall off. Ticks are usually found on your dog's underside, under the forelegs, and on the head. Your dog is most likely to pick up ticks in wooded areas during spring and summer.

Ticks can carry serious diseases, such as Rocky Mountain Spotted Fever and Lyme disease. Cases of Lyme disease have been reported in the United States along the East coast, in the Midwest and in northern California. Ticks carrying Lyme disease can cause lameness, arthritis and kidney or heart disease in your dog. The bite of an infected tick can also cause illness in humans.

During the warm weather, you should check for ticks daily. They are easily seen on short-haired dogs, looking like small, dark spots. On long-haired dogs, you will need to run your hand carefully through the dog's coat so you don't overlook any ticks. To remove a tick, use a pair of tweezers to pull the tick from the dog's skin. Grasp the tick near its head—it's important to remove the head, otherwise an infection can occur. Some authorities recommend first dabbing the tick with alcohol to kill, or at least relax, the tick, making it easier to remove the head. Wearing gloves helps prevent the spread of infection.

Flea sprays and dips help to prevent ticks, but be sure to consult your veterinarian about the proper treatment. If you are already treating your dog for fleas, the combined treatment for both fleas and ticks can prove harmful to your dog by overwhelming it with too many insecticides.

LICE. There are two varieties of lice. Biting lice chew on your dog's skin, while sucking lice penetrate the skin and feed on tissue fluids. Lice are small and gray, and lay tiny clusters of eggs that can be seen on the dog's hair. They are harmful and should be treated promptly with sprays, baths or dips. Your veterinarian can suggest the most effective treatment.

MITES. Mange, a serious skin disease, is caused by mites, extremely small parasites no larger than a pinhead. There are two forms of mange: sarcoptic and demodectic. A dog infected with sarcoptic mange will scratch and chew at its skin. The affected area is red and full of bloody sores and scabs. Eventually, the hair sheds, leaving the affected area bare. As the disease spreads, you can detect a harsh odor. The symptoms of demodectic mange are similar, but less severe. There may only a slight loss of hair and some reddening and inflammation of the affected area. This condition causes less itching and irritation than sarcoptic mange. The only signs may be a small lesion marked by hair loss or a small bald spot. The sarcoptic variety is highly contagious, but both forms require treatment.

Ear mites can also infect your dog, causing it to shake or scratch its head. Check the ears for dark earwax, and take your dog to the vet if you suspect ear mites.

RINGWORM. Ringworm is not a worm, but a fungus that grows on the skin. The signs resemble mange—look for irritated, scaly, inflamed skin. Ringworm can infect humans, so prompt treatment is essential. Treatment includes iodine shampoos, clipping the affected area, creams and oral medication.

At top: Some of the common parasites that affect dogs. *Above:* When examining your dog's ears check for dark earwax, a sign of ear mites. *Right:* Flea shampoos are one method of getting rid of fleas. Other products include sprays, powders and dips. *Facing page:* A well-trained (and well-groomed) Standard Poodle.

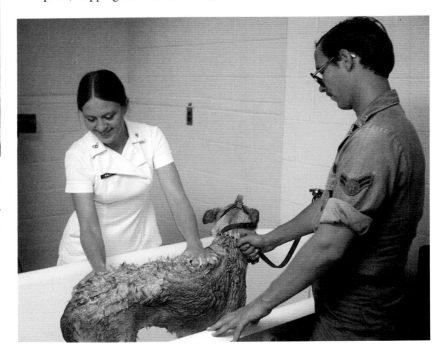

THE PICTORIAL GUIDE TO DOG CARE

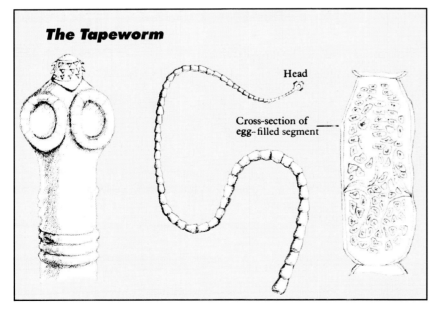

The Tapeworm

Head

Cross-section of
egg-filled segment

**At top: A young woman and her English Setter enjoy a game of fetch.
Above: Tapeworms are one of the most common internal parasites
affecting dogs.**

Internal Parasites

Many dogs will have worms at some point in their lives, often at the puppy stage. In general, the symptoms are listlessness, diarrhea, weight loss and a bloated abdomen. If you suspect that your dog has worms, take a stool sample to the veterinarian for diagnosis. Although there are over-the-counter worm treatments, they are not as effective as those prescribed by the veterinarian.

ROUNDWORMS. There are several varieties of roundworms, the most common of which are ascarids. Some varieties live in your dog's small intestine; others infest the large intestine, blood vessels and respiratory tract. The adult worm, which is sometimes visible in your dog's stool, can be up to four or five inches long.

Roundworms are especially harmful to puppies. The worms move through the body causing vomiting, diarrhea, dehydration, pneumonia or stunted growth. Infected puppies frequently exhibit a potbelly, and may develop pneumonia or hepatitis.

As the puppy grows older, the worms travel to the muscles where they form cysts. The worms lie dormant until the puppy (if female) becomes pregnant and are then transmitted to the lungs of the embryo puppies. Because the chance of your puppy being born with roundworms is fairly high, it is a good idea to take a stool sample to the vet when your puppy receives its first series of inoculations.

TAPEWORMS. Tapeworms enter your dog's digestive system through larvae transmitted by fleas, rodents and rabbits. As the worms mature, they feed from the dog's intestine, causing it to eat more than normal without any weight gain. The worm attaches its head to the small intestine, where it will grow into a long

chain of segments. These segments, which look like rice, break off and can be seen in the dog's stool, beneath its tail, or in its bedding. Treatment must involve getting rid of fleas, otherwise your dog will likely be reinfected.

HOOKWORMS. Hookworms attach themselves to the walls of the small intestine. An adult dog contracts hookworms when it ingests larvae or when larvae penetrates its skin. Puppies can be infected when larvae is transmitted through the mother's placenta or her milk. Signs of hookworms include listlessness, poor appetite, weight loss and black or bloody stools. These worms can cause diarrhea or anemia, which can be fatal if not treated.

Hookworms are not visible to the eye; a veterinarian must examine a stool sample microscopically. Following treatment, keep your dog away from an area that be contaminated with infected dog feces.

HEARTWORMS. Unlike most internal parasites, which affect the intestines, heartworms attach themselves to the heart and lungs. The larvae are transmitted by mosquitoes. When a mosquito bites a dog, the larvae enter the bloodstream, where it will take about six months for the mature worm to develop.

Heartworm disease is very serious and can be fatal if not treated. Dogs with heartworm disease can recover if the infestation is discovered early. However, the treatment is complex and not without complications. The best cure is prevention and, fortunately, medication in the form of a monthly pill is now available to combat this disease. Your dog will stay on the medication during the mosquito season, although in warm climates, your veterinarian may recommend the medication year-round. Before starting your dog on this medication, your veterinarian will take a blood test to ensure that the dog is free from heartworm disease.

At top: The Walker Coonhound is one of the many varieties of coonhounds. Above: Pet stores offer a wide array of products to combat fleas.

FIGHTING YOUR DOG'S PARASITES

Caring For Your Dog's Teeth, Nails And Ears

Dental Care

Proper dental care is one of the most neglected aspects of pet care. Neglecting your dog's teeth can lead not only to diseases of the mouth and tooth loss but also to infections elsewhere in the body. Signs of dental disease include reluctance to eat, drooling, blood in the saliva, yellow-brown tartar at the gumline, broken teeth and extremely bad breath.

As in humans, tartar accumulation causes periodontal (gum) disease. In the early stages of the disease, the gums become infected and inflamed. Plaque, a bacteria-laden film, forms on the teeth. The bacteria infects the gum tissue and then the roots of the teeth. The bones underlying the teeth begin to erode, the gums recede, and eventually the teeth fall out.

An amazing number of dogs suffer from periodontal disease—yet it is one of the most preventable diseases. You can help reduce tartar build-up by giving your dog dry food or dog biscuits. The best strategy, however, is brushing your dog's teeth. The idea of brushing your dog's teeth may sound ridiculous, but proper dental care is just as important for your dog as it is for you. When your dog is a puppy, massage its gums so it becomes accustomed to your hands in its mouth. To clean your dog's teeth, use a soft child's toothbrush or one that is designed especially for pets, and brush the teeth just as you would brush your own. Special toothpastes are also available, or you can use baking soda. Whatever you do, don't use toothpastes made for humans—they may make your dog gag. Besides, most dogs don't like the taste. Some vets recommend brushing your dog's teeth every other day; others suggest once a week.

Heavy accumulation of tartar may have to be removed under an anesthetic, which is costly for you and uncomfortable for your dog. So brush your dog's teeth and avoid this procedure if you can.

Facing page: A dog having its teeth cleaned. The procedure is costly and must be performed under an anesthetic, but can be avoided if you clean your dog's teeth on a regular basis.

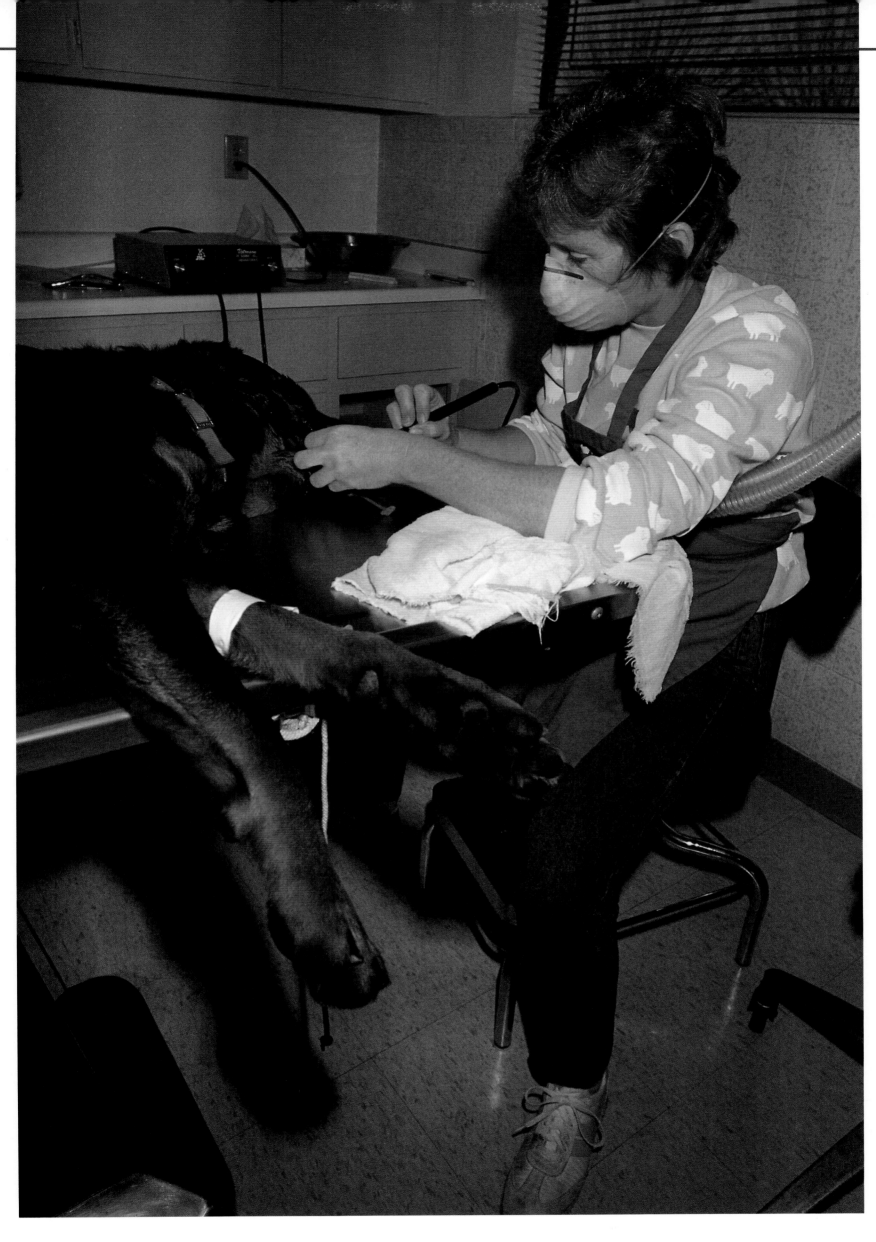

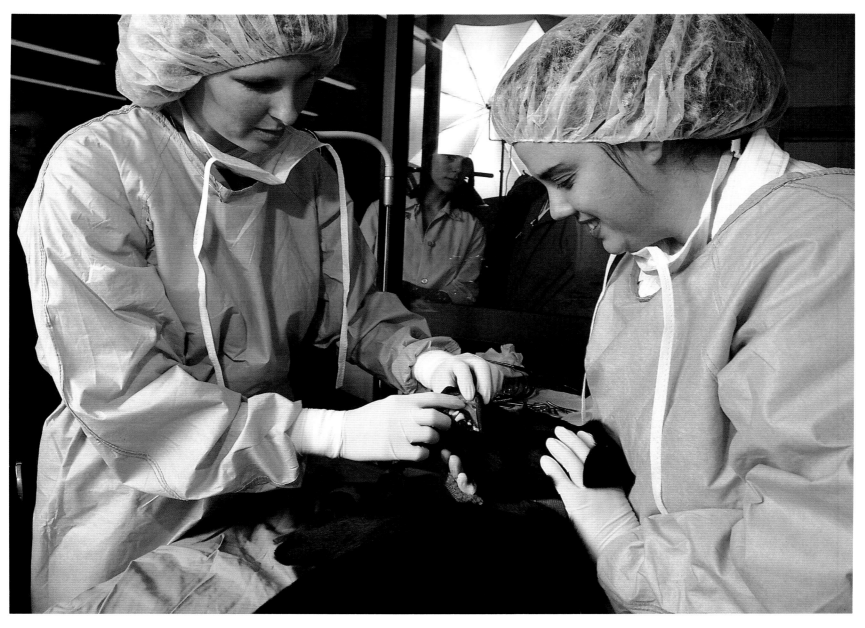

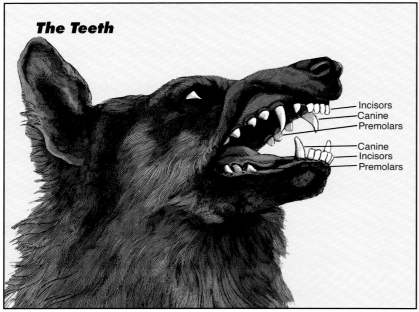

The Teeth

Incisors
Canine
Premolars
Canine
Incisors
Premolars

At top: Periodontal disease is a common, but preventable, ailment. *Above:* The dog's teeth. Not seen in the diagram are carnassials and molars. *Right:* A Doberman has his teeth examined. *Far right:* Puppies need a variety of chew toys while they are teething. *Facing page, above:* Dogs with long ear flaps are more prone to ear problems than dogs with erect ears because the flaps reduce ventilation, which can lead to an infection if excess wax forms.

Dogs can suffer from other dental problems, too. Chewing on sharp objects—sticks, rocks, wall, fences, bones—can break your dog's teeth. A cracked or broken tooth is a breeding ground for infection. If your dog has a swollen jaw, it may be a sign of infection in the root of a tooth. If not treated, the infection can spread to the jawbone and throughout the bloodstream.

Nail Care

At some point, you will need to trim your dog's nails. The pavement helps to wear down the nail, but dogs that spend a lot of time indoors will need their nails trimmed fairly often. If you have never trimmed a dog's nails, it is a good idea to have a groomer or vet show you how. Guillotine-type clippers are good to use because they cut the nail, unlike plier-type clippers which can crush the nail.

Be sure not to clip the quick of the nail (the blood vessel that runs through the nail). The quick has a nerve-ending and, in addition to bleeding, will hurt your dog if cut. You can easily see the quick on dogs with white nails, but it narrows at the end, becoming harder to see, so you will need to compensate for this. If you do draw blood, stop the bleeding with a styptic pencil. Be sure to check the dew claw (if present). These claws won't wear down on their own and can easily become ingrown if neglected.

The quick grows along with the nail. If you let the nail grow too long, you may end up cutting the quick to get the nail to a reasonable length.

Ear Care

On a regular basis—every day or so if possible—examine your dog's ears. Like dental care, this is a good practice to establish when your dog is a puppy.

Begin the exam by looking inside the dog's ear. The surface of the ear canal should be clean and have a similar appearance to the hairless part of the dog's belly. A little ear wax is normal, but if wax or hair is blocking the ear, it should be cleaned/plucked. Warning: Don't attempt to clean your dog's ears unless your vet has shown you how. If the ear has an unpleasant odor, consult your vet—this could be a sign of infection. When the daily ear exam is over, tell your dog what a wonderful and cooperative dog it has been.

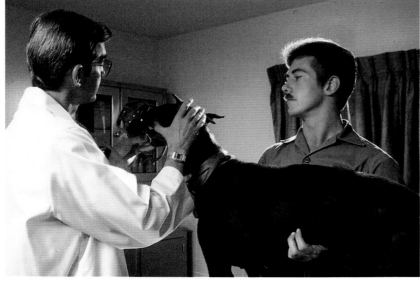

CARING FOR YOUR DOG'S TEETH, NAILS AND EARS

Grooming Your Dog

Because the different breeds have such a wide variety of coat types, some dogs are obviously easier to care for than others. Ease of grooming is something to consider before you make a decision to purchase a dog. Old English Sheepdogs, Collies and Afghan Hounds clearly require more grooming time than the sleek-haired Beagle. As much as an hour a day is needed to thoroughly groom the thick coat of the Old English Sheepdog.

Grooming your dog is part of being a responsible owner. Brushing your dog not only keeps it looking and feeling its best, it also can alert you to health problems—such as ear or skin disorders. Grooming removes the dead hair, while cleaning the living hair and skin.

Grooming necessities are a comb and a brush, but scissors also come in handy. Select a brush that is appropriate for your dog's coat, making sure that the bristles are long enough to reach through the coat. Wide-toothed combs are handy for breaking up mats and tangles, while fine-toothed combs separate the undercoat, bringing out the dead hair. Fine-toothed combs are useful under the chin and tail and behind the ears and are a necessity during flea season. As you comb your dog, you can catch the offending fleas and then drown them in a cup of water.

To groom a long-haired dog with an undercoat (Collie, Newfoundland), use your wide-toothed comb on the tangles. Brush and comb the coat forward over the head and shoulders before combing it back. Brush the flanks following the lay of the coat. You will need a brush with long, wide-set bristles. If possible, bathe these dogs only twice a year.

Dogs with long silky coats, such as Afghans, Yorkies and spaniels, need frequent brushing to avoid matting. Be sure to use a brush with long enough bristles, or you'll end up grooming only the outer coat. These dogs require more frequent baths than other long-haired dogs.

Wire-haired dogs (most terriers) need regular combing to avoid mats. They should be stripped or plucked every three to four months, and for this you will need a stripping or plucking comb. An easier method is to have the dog professionally clipped by a groomer.

***Facing page:* The long coat of the Bearded Collie requires regular brushing, especially during shedding season.**

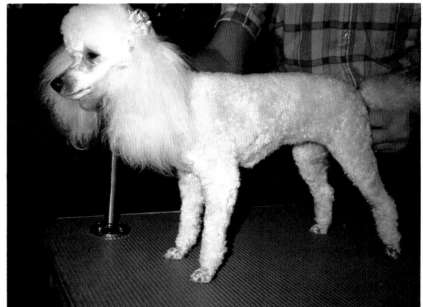

Shampoos *(at top)* and clippers *(above)* are the basic tools of professional groomers. These products are also available for the nonprofessional. *Right, top to bottom:* A groomer trims a Poodle — and the finished product. *Facing page, above:* Even the short-coated Basset Hound needs to be brushed. *Facing page, below:* Most dogs enjoy being brushed and will stand still while being groomed.

Short-haired dogs are the easiest to groom. For dogs with a short, fine co like a Boxer, all you will need is a 'houndglove.' Dogs with a slightly longer c (Labrador, Golden Retriever) will need combing and brushing. A slicker bru (a rectangular brush with bent, wire bristles) is an ideal tool for removing t dead hair of the undercoat.

Curly-coated dogs require clippings every six weeks or so. A puppy's first c will be needed at about 14 weeks. Comb and brush the coat every few days

Use blunt-edged scissors to trim your dog's hair in delicate places. (occasion, you will need to trim the hair around the eyes of your Old Engli Sheepdog or Maltese. Spaniels need trimming between the pads of their feet a on their ear flaps to prevent hair from blocking the ear canal. In some case, y will want to trim a few straggly hairs for appearance's sake. Never trim yo dog's whiskers.

Shedding

Dogs, with the exception of the curly-coated breeds, shed heavily twice a year—in the spring and fall. Shedding lasts about a month. This pattern varies tremendously depending on the area of the country and the local weather conditions. The new coat will grow in in three to four months. During the shedding season, brush your dog daily.

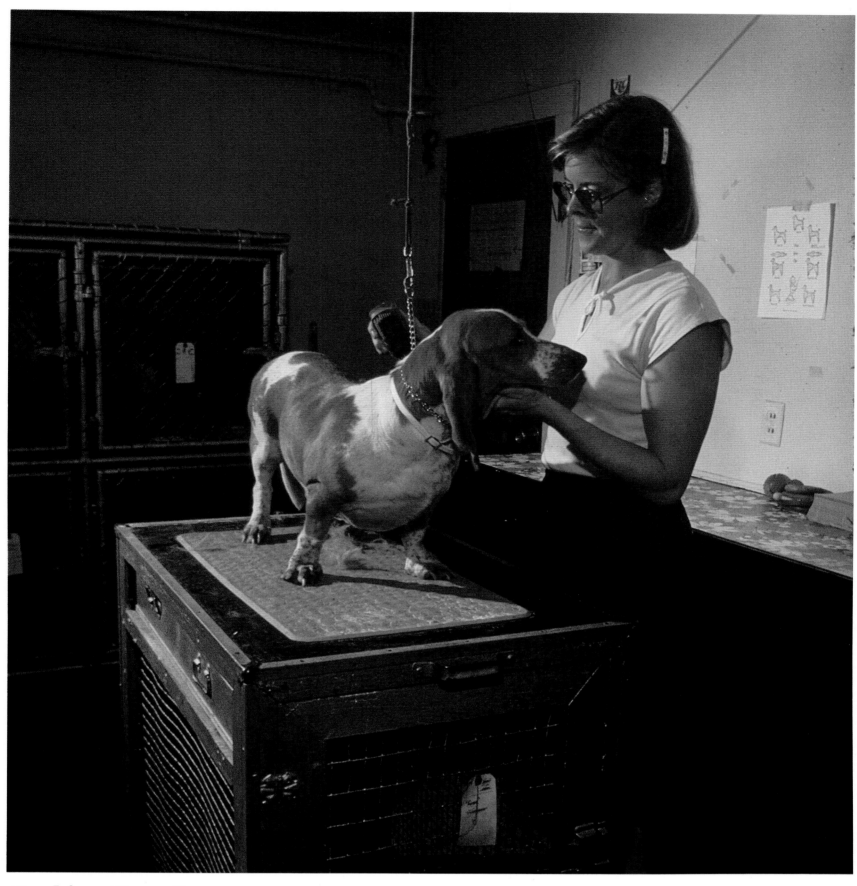

Bathing Your Dog

As a general rule of thumb, dogs need to be bathed about once a month. Some authorities caution against bathing a dog too much because it dries out the skin out or promotes shedding of the undercoat, but the bottom line is bathe your dog when it is dirty! The size of your dog dictates the best place to bathe it. A small dog fits nicely in the kitchen sink or a baby bathtub. Large dogs will need a large area—a wading pool or maybe just the garden hose in the backyard providing the weather is warm, but many dogs end up in their owners' bathtubs.

Begin by placing the dog in the bathtub. Use a pitcher or hose to wet it down, starting at the back and working toward the head. Make sure the water is warm. Use a dog shampoo or a mild shampoo for people. Apply the shampoo in the same manner as you did the water, leaving the head for last. However, when you rinse the dog, begin at the head, working back. Squeeze out excess water and towel dry the dog. For puppies and toy dogs, you can use a hair dryer—but use it with caution, the noise may frighten the dog. Unless your puppy has fleas or is really dirty, don't bathe it until it is six months old.

GROOMING YOUR DOG

Neutering Your Dog

Spaying

If you do not plan to breed your female dog, it is a good idea to have her spayed. Spaying is the surgical removal of the ovaries and uterus. This routine operation guarantees that your pet will not become pregnant. A spayed dog will not go into heat, which can be uncomfortable for her and inconvenient for you. Male dogs are attracted to a female in heat and will gather around your door. Inconvenience aside, studies have shown that spaying reduces the risk of breast cancer, and, of course, the chance of uterine infection or cancer is completely eliminated. If you are having trouble deciding whether or not to spay your dog, think of all the unwanted dogs that humane societies put to sleep every year. Many of them are unplanned puppies.

Your puppy should be spayed before she goes into her first heat—at about six months of age. Larger breeds mature later, so wait until she reaches eight months. Dogs spayed at an early age recover quickly. The operation is performed under a general anesthetic. Your vet may want to keep the dog overnight for observation, but in many cases you will be able to take your pet home the same day. Some vets use stitches that dissolve, in which case you will not have to go back to the vet to have the stitches removed.

Castration

Although many people neuter their male cats, some people seem to have a psychological objection to neutering a male dog, and yet the reasons for and results of castration are the same for both dog and cat: A neutered male will have less desire to wander. Neutering your pet will not change your dog's personality, but it will help to discourage overly aggressive behavior, hyperactivity and indoor urination. Contrary to popular belief, neutering your dog will not make him (or her) overweight. Dogs gain weight because their owners feed them too much.

Like a female dog, a male dog should be neutered before he reaches sexual maturity, typically six to eight months of age. Your pet will recover rapidly from the surgery, but he may have to stay overnight at the hospital.

Facing page: A dog is readied for surgery. Veterinarians recommend you neuter your dog when it is about six months old.

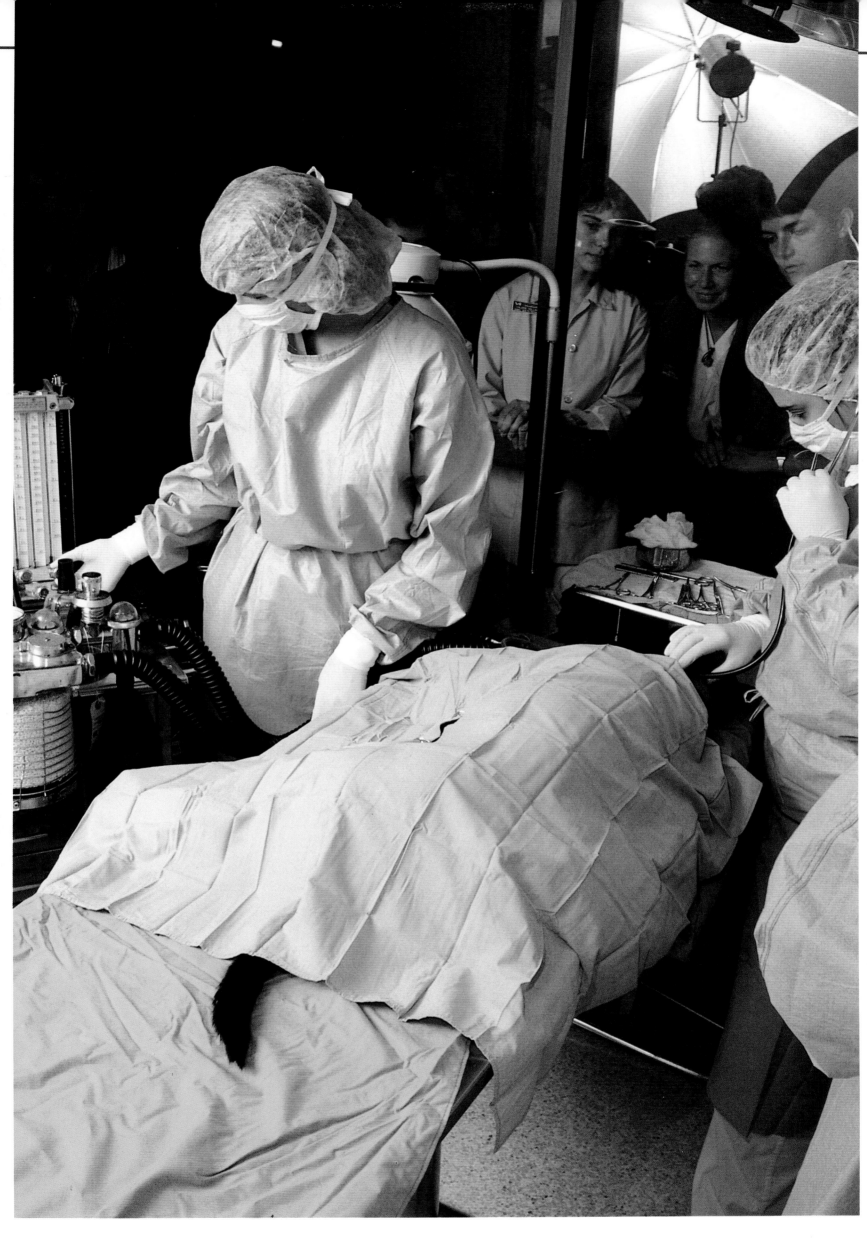

Caring For Your Aging Dog

Like humans, dogs experience physical changes as they grow older. As your dog ages, its body functions less efficiently, which increases the risk of infection and other problems. Different breeds of dogs age at different speeds. In general, large breeds age the quickest. Very large breeds such as Great Danes and St Bernards may show signs of age as early as six years of age, and many don't live beyond ten years. Few Labrador Retrievers will last beyond 14 years, but small dogs can live more than 20 years.

The most common signs of aging are gray hair around the head, especially the muzzle and ears, and weight gain or loss. Your dog may also show a decrease in activity, loss of hearing, and changes in mood or temperament.

An old dog isn't necessarily an unhealthy dog, but you should watch for signs of trouble. Call your vet if your dog shows any of these signs:

1. A sudden weight gain or loss. Weight loss is usually associated with liver or kidney problems.

2. Excessive thirst.

3. A sudden change in bowel habits. Constipation in old male dogs may be the result of prostate problems.

4. Frequent urination. Frequent urination, sometimes accompanied by excessive thirst, may signal kidney problems. Medication and a change in diet as prescribed by your vet may help to alleviate the problem.

5. Stiff joints. Stiff joints and/or limping are signals of arthritis, which is more common in large or overweight dogs.

6. Coughing. Coughing, shortness of breath and a tendency to tire easily are signs of heart disease.

7. Bad breath. Bad breath is a sign of peritonital, or gum, disease. Brushing your dogs teeth will help to remove tartar build-up. In severe cases, tartar may need to be removed under an anaesthetic. Bad breath can also signal kidney failure.

Loss of hearing and sight are a consequence of age, and many dogs can function well despite these disabilities. You can tell your dog is losing its hearing if it barks for no reason or if it ignores you. The hard-of-hearing dog

Facing page: As your dog ages, you need to be aware of the signs of illness (see text above). An annual visit to the vet is a good precaution.

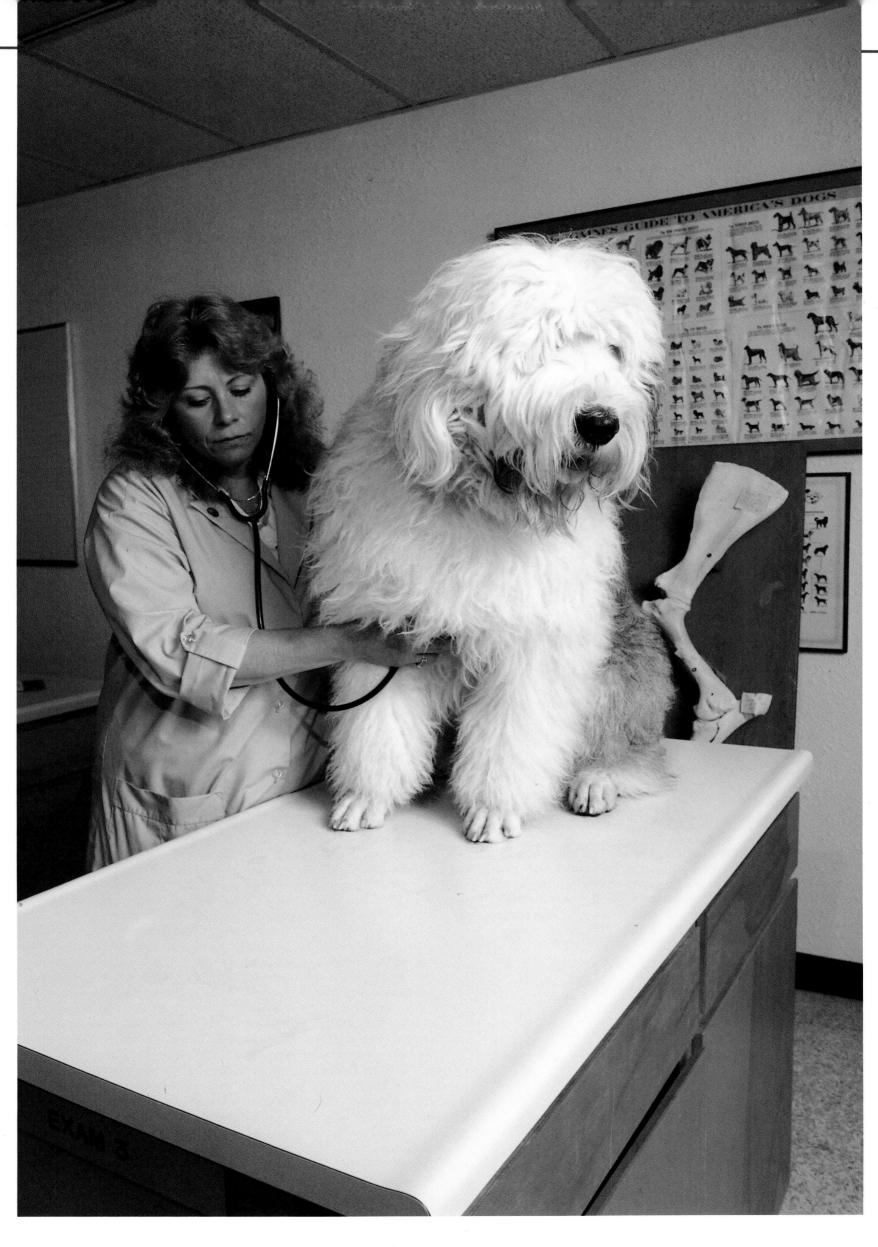

Above: Growing old together. Dogs of any age make good companions for young and old *(facing page)* alike. Studies have shown that people recover more quickly if they have contact with a pet, and some hospitals have programs in which dogs visit the patients. Health care experts find this improves morale and in turn aids in recovery.

should not be allowed to wander, for it may be deaf to signs of danger—such as a honking horn. Take care not to startle the dog that is losing its sight. For example, make sure it sees you before you turn on the vacuum cleaner. If your dog goes blind, its sense of hearing and smell may compensate for the loss of sight. You can help your dog by not rearranging the furniture.

A dog in its twilight years values a routine. You should try to feed and walk it at the same time every day. A change in the routine can be stressful to the older dog, and stress will adversely affect its health. Although your dog may have accompanied you on your vacation in its younger years, it will probably be more comfortable in its own surroundings, with a neighbor taking care of it.

You can keep the older dog healthy by watching its diet. Your dog will need less food than it did in its youth. In addition, its physical condition, such as kidney or liver problems, may dictate a special diet. Exercise is still important, but moderate the amount. As always, brush your dog regularly.

Health care for animals has advanced incredibly in the last few years, and many of the medical procedures that help people can benefit your dog, too. Pacemakers and contact lenses are now available for dogs, and some veterinary hospitals treat cancer with chemotherapy and immunotherapy.

In spite of your best care, if your dog's health declines severely, your vet may recommend that it be euthanized, or put to sleep. Euthanasia is usually an injection of a large overdose of an anesthetic. The process is fast and painless, and, if you want, can be performed as you hold your dog. Losing a dog is losing a loved one, and you should allow yourself time to feel grief over your pet's death.

THE PICTORIAL GUIDE TO DOG CARE

First Aid For Your Dog

Everyday life is filled with hazards—both major and minor. A dog can chew on an electrical cord and go into shock, it may eat antifreeze and poison itself, or it may be hit by a car. All of these situations require the immediate attention of a veterinarian, but the few steps you take before the vet can see your dog may mean the difference between life and death.

A first aid kit equipped with the following items will help you handle an emergency situation:
- Tweezers—For removing splinters and glass.
- Rectal thermometer.
- Eyedropper—For liquid medicine.
- Cotton—For wrapping sprains.
- Gauze Bandages—Pads for dressing wounds and rolls for muzzling an injured dog.
- Hydrogen peroxide solution (three percent)—To wash minor wounds and to induce vomiting.

Emergency Situations

ALLERGIC REACTIONS. Insect bites may produce itching or tearing eyes, a swollen face, difficulty breathing and, in severe cases, collapse and unconsciousness. If your dog has collapsed, rush it to the vet.

BITES. If your dog is bitten by another dog, or even a cat, the first thing to do is locate the source of the wound. If necessary, clip away the hair. To stop the blood loss, apply direct pressure to the wound with your hand or a pressure bandage. If bleeding continues, apply a gauze pad, using strips of gauze to wrap it tightly. If the bleeding is severe, you may have to use a tourniquet. Wrap a length of gauze or other material twice around the dog between the wound and the heart and tighten enough to stop the bleeding. A tourniquet should only be used as a last resort—it can cause nerve damage or loss of the limb if left in place too long. A pressure bandage is usually more effective and much safer. Loosen the tourniquet every five to 10 minutes if your vet is more than 15 or 20 minutes away.

Facing page: Every day veterinarians handle emergency situations — from bites and wounds from a dog fight to bee stings to car accidents.

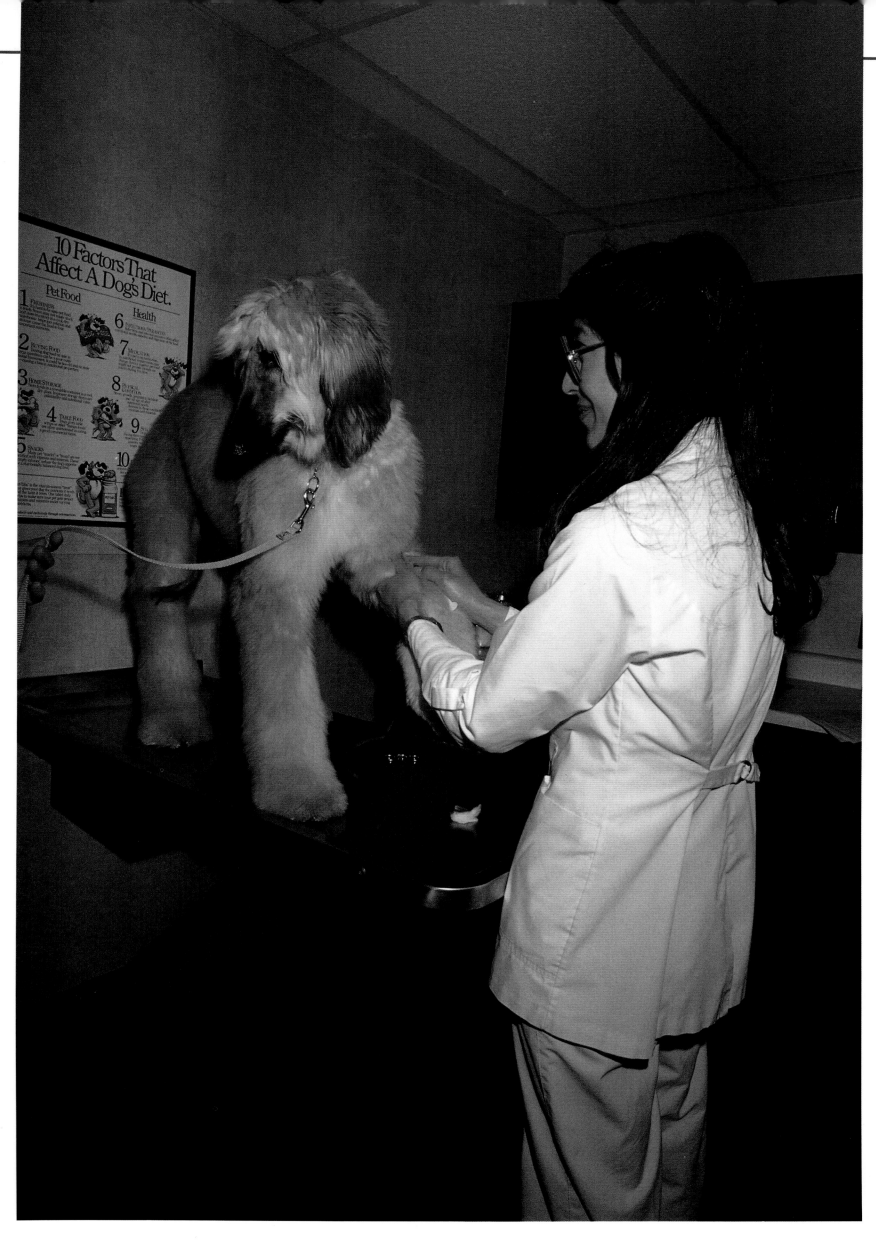

FIRST AID FOR YOUR DOG

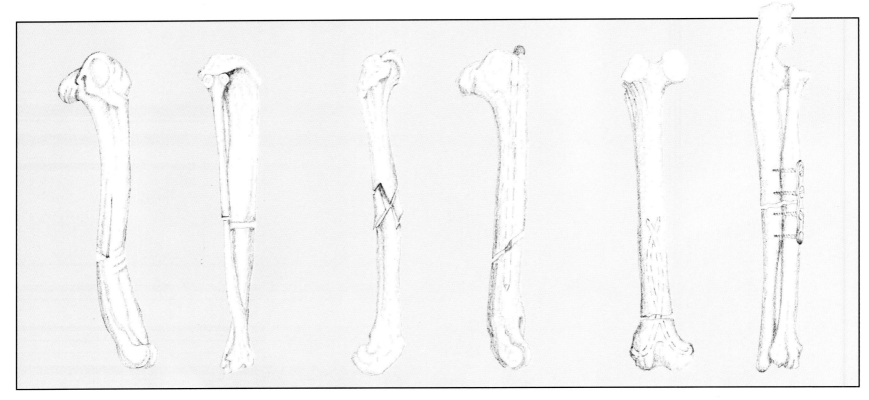

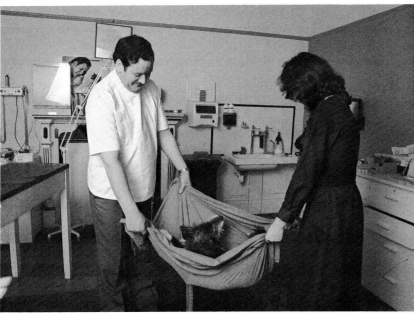

At top, from left to right: **The first three illustrations show the different ways a bone can break—a greenstick fracture, a clean break and a break with splinters. The next three illustrations show how bones can be mended—single pinning, double rush-type pins for a fracture of the femur and a bone plate repair of the radius and ulna.** *Above:* **Moving an injured dog.**

BURNS. Apply cold water or ice to the burned area. Anything else could cause an infection. Rush your dog to the vet.

CAR ACCIDENT. If your dog is hit by a car, approach it cautiously and speak to it reassuringly. Check its heartbeat and breathing and look for wounds and fracture. Call your vet's office so that he can prepare for your arrival.

In some cases (if the dog is trapped under the car, for example) a veterinarian will have to deal with the injured dog at the site of the accident. In general, however, it is best to get the dog to the vet as soon as possible.

CHOKING. A stick or small ball can get stuck in your dog's throat. Push the lower jaw open and tilt the head. If possible, remove the object with your fingers. If that does not work, kneel behind the dog, holding its body just below the ribs. Squeeze hard a few times. If the object does not pop out, take your dog to the vet immediately.

DROWNING. First empty the dog's lungs of water. For a small dog, pick it up by the back legs and hold it upside down for 10 to 15 seconds. For a large dog, pick it up behind the ribs, with one arm around the abdomen, and drape the dog over your shoulder. Then administer artificial respiration. If there's no heartbeat, also give CPR (cardiopulmonary resuscitation) *if you know how.* Wrap the dog in a blanket to prevent shock.

ELECTRIC SHOCK. Using a wooden object, knock the electrical cord from the socket. Cover the dog with a blanket, and if needed apply artificial respiration and CPR.

FRACTURE. Restrict your dog's movement and apply a splint to the fractured leg if you are very far from a veterinarian. If you have cotton wool, wrap it twice around the length of the leg. Once the leg is covered, lay two sticks (a rolled newspaper will work in a pinch) on either side of the leg and hold them in place with gauze or a bandage. *An improperly applied splint can do more harm than good, so only attempt this if you have the necessary training and experience.*

HEATSTROKE. Heatstroke is caused by high heat and humidity and lack of water and ventilation. It frequently results when a dog is left in a car during hot weather. Signs include panting, high fever, frothing at the mouth, shock and collapse. Lower the dog's temperature by immersing it in cold water up to the neck or spraying it with cold water. Apply an ice pack to the dog's head and take it to the vet.

POISONING. Common symptoms of poisoning are stomach pains, howling, whimpering, diarrhea, convulsions, tremors and labored breathing. Many poisons are fatal if not treated immediately. Contact your veterinarian. If you know what the dog has swallowed, your vet may tell you to induce vomiting with an emetic, such as hydrogen peroxide solution or syrup of ipecac. To give your dog liquid medicine, fill a plastic eyedropper or spoon with the liquid and pull the dog's lip at the cheek to form a pouch. Fill the pouch with the liquid.

Dogs are frequently poisoned by rodent poison, pesticides and antifreeze.

THE PICTORIAL GUIDE TO DOG CARE

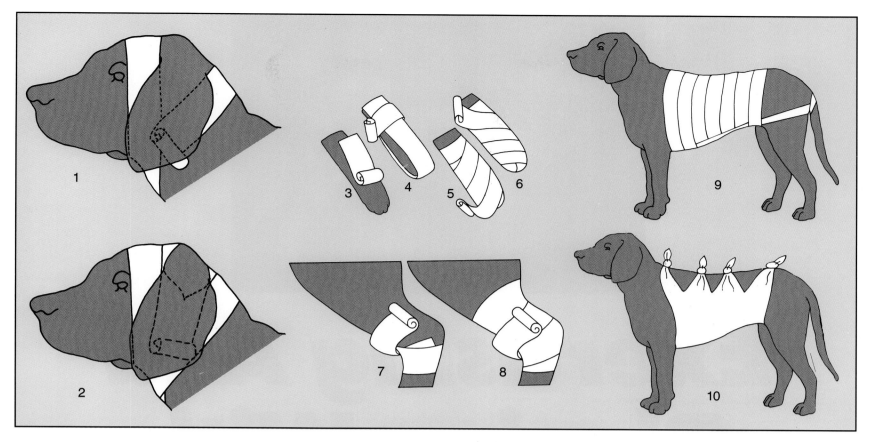

SHOCK.

Shock often follows some kind of traumatic situation, such as a car accident. A dog in shock may appear to be asleep, or it may be semiconscious. Symptoms vary according to the severity of condition. Your dog's breathing may be shallow, its body may be cold, and its pulse rapid. Gums that are white instead of pink are an important clue.

If your dog is in shock, try to calm it and keep it warm. Its actions may be unpredictable, so use caution in handling it. Take the dog to the vet immediately.

SPRAINS.

Large breeds in particular are prone to sprains. First, apply a cold compress—a cloth soaked in chilled water. Apply a fresh compress every 20 minutes. After a few hours, switch to a hot compress. If lameness persists for more than 24 hours, an examination by your veterinarian and possibly an X-ray will be indicated.

SWALLOWED OBJECTS.

If the dog has swallowed any unnatural object, it is best to take it immediately to the veterinarian. Do not try to induce vomiting. An X-ray examination will help to determine the need for surgical removal.

Emergency Techniques

ADMINISTERING ARTIFICIAL RESPIRATION. Lay the dog on its side and check to see that the airway is free from obstructions. Place your mouth over the dog's mouth and nose. Exhale until the dog's chest expands. Remove your mouth. Repeat the step when the chest falls. When the dog starts to breathe on its own, rush it to the veterinarian.

GIVING CPR (CARDIOPULMONARY RESPIRATION). CPR is necessary if your dog's heart stops following an accident. Place the heel of one hand on the dog's chest. Place your other hand palm down on top. Press firmly; release; pause. Repeat 20 or 30 times a minute. Take care not to bruise or break the dog's ribs. Take the dog to the vet when its heart starts beating on its own.

MUZZLING YOUR DOG. An injured dog may attempt to bite its owner out of fear. To protect yourself, muzzle it with a tie or long strip of gauze. To muzzle it, slip a loop over its nose. Knot the loop on top and again under the jaw. Tie the ends behind the ears. Loosen the muzzle if the dog turns blue or starts to have trouble breathing.

Never muzzle a dog that is choking or one that is having trouble breathing.
Never leave a muzzled dog alone.
Never muzzle a short-nosed breed—it may have problems breathing.

MOVING AN INJURED DOG. Gently slide the dog onto a blanket, jacket, ironing board or some kind of makeshift stretcher. If possible, three people are needed to support the head, body and pelvis. If a stretcher isn't available, carry your dog. Support a small dog in the crook of your arm; hold a large dog across your arms with each arm inside its front and hind legs.

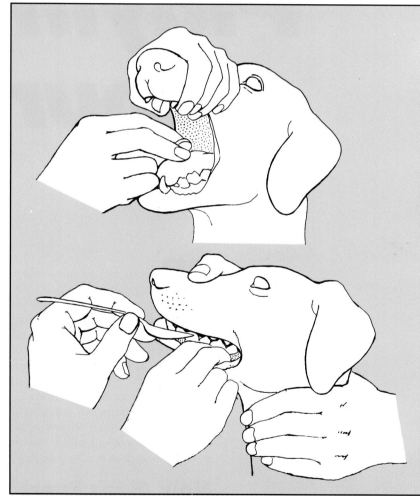

At top: **Bandage the head (1) in a figure eight, wrapping the bandage under each ear (2). A paw can be bandaged by laying a gauze strip down one side (3) and up the other (4). Then spiral the bandage down one side (5) and back up the other side (6). To bandage an injured leg, wrap the gauze around the wound (7) and secure the bandage above the joint (8). To bandage the abdomen, wrap the bandage around the wound several times (9) and secure it around the tail, or use a many-tailed bandage (10).** *Above:* **To administer pills (top), open the dog's mouth by raising its upper jaw. Place the pill on the back of the tongue. Close the mouth and massage the throat to encourage swallowing. To administer liquid medicine (bottom), hold the dog's upper jaw and pour the liquid into the pouch formed by the side of the lower lip. Give only a small amount at a time and allow the dog to swallow.**

Exercising And Playing With Your Dog

Exercise is essential to your dog's health and well-being. Not only does daily exercise promote strong cardiovascular health, it also creates an important bond between you and your dog. By nature dogs are pack animals and crave companionship. In the wild, wolves—the dog's cousin—frolic with their siblings and other pack members. Many dogs today, however, are left alone all day while their owners are at work. Even if you leave your dog with plenty of toys and a large back yard to run around in chances are it will not exercise as much as it needs to. You are your dog's best playmate.

When you come home from work, you may want to sit down and relax, but your dog, thrilled to see you after your long absence, will want to play. An evening walk or a game of fetch in the backyard are two good ways to combine exercise with companionship. Playing fetch or frisbee with your dog has the added advantage of honing your dog's motor skills.

How Much Exercise?

How much exercise your dog needs depends on its size and breed. Common sense tells you that a large breed requires much more exercise than a toy breed, but size can be deceiving—a small terrier, such as the Norfolk Terrier, enjoys a good romp and needs more exercise than you would think when judging by appearance alone.

If you are an avid jogger, you will probably want to take your dog with when you jog. If you have a large dog, it will enjoy jogging with you, but keep in mind that a dog, like a person, needs to work up a to given amount of exercise. Dogs were not meant to be marathon runners, so don't take your dog for an overly long run. Watch for signs of fatigue. If your dog appears tired—STOP. This is true of

Facing page: Caring for a dog means giving it the exercise it needs—even in the rain.

THE PICTORIAL GUIDE TO DOG CARE

EXERCISING AND PLAYING WITH YOUR DOG

any kind of exercise. Some puppies will want to play to the point of exhaustion, but their bones and muscles are still developing and can be damaged through over-exercising. Large breeds especially should never be exercised to the point of exhaustion during their first year of life.

Toys

Dogs, adults and puppies alike, need toys. When you are away, toys will ease the boredom of being left alone. Some dogs resort to chewing bedroom slippers when their owners are away, and puppies can wreak havoc on your shoes or furniture while they are teething. Fortunately, dogs are intelligent animals and can be taught to chew on their toys rather than your belongings.

Pet stores and even grocery stores have shelves filled with all sorts of dog toys, but perhaps one of the best toys around is the tennis ball. A tennis ball is large enough that it won't lodge in the throat of most breeds, and still small enough that even a smaller dog can get a good grip on it. But a tennis ball in a sock (an old sweat sock is the best choice) is a toy made in heaven. You and your dog will enjoy hours of tug-of-war with the tennis ball/sock toy.

Play With Me

You can tell your dog wants to play when it crouches down, its rump in the air, tail wagging. It will probably bark and may reach out with its paw. It will run back and then reapproach you. Its mouth will be partially open, and its expression will look like a grin.

Above: Since most dogs love to retrieve, a game of fetch is an excellent way to exercise your dog. *Above, right:* A Rottweiler in a playful mood. No matter how old, dogs enjoy playing with toys *(right)*. *Facing page:* Summertime fun—a boy, a dog, a frisbee and an ocean.

THE PICTORIAL GUIDE TO DOG CARE

Training Your Dog

The dog has been man's companion through the ages. This centuries old friendship is due, in part, to the dog's ability to be trained. Dogs are pack animals and will instinctively follow the orders of the leader of the pack—the owner. Dogs are intelligent animals. Scientists and lay people alike debate the issue of the dog's intelligence, for which there is no easy answer. Dogs cannot think like humans do, but they are capable of understanding quite a lot. Simple phrases and words are not beyond a dog's understanding, as many dog owners can testify—'Jason, eat your crunchies' or 'Sarah, go to sleep.' How does the dog understand? A dog owner might argue that a dog has the mind of a small child, while others contend that the dog has simply learned the command. Some people measure a dog's intelligence by how quickly it learns; others might point to a dog's ability to sense its owner's mood as a sign of intelligence.

Dogs, like people, learn at different rates, but with a little patience and consistency, all dogs, with few exceptions, should be trained to come when called, to walk calmly beside their masters, to lie down quietly and obediently. A well trained dog will not beg from the table; it won't destroy the furniture in your living room or the roses in your garden.

Although dogs can be easily trained, training a dog requires commitment on the owner's part. A dog needs frequent lessons; a training session every other week will not be enough to train a dog. A human being could not learn how to play the piano if he sat down for twenty minutes once a week. Only through repetition, firmness and consistency will your dog learn. Tone of voice conveys much to your dog. When you want it to come or play fetch, generate some excitement with your voice. When you want it to heel or to stop chewing on your Italian leather shoes, use a firm voice. A conversational tone will get you nowhere. Some people, particularly women, have a difficult time learning to project a powerful tone of voice. For these people, hand signals used in conjunction with voice commands effectively convey a sense of authority to the dog.

Dogs want to please. Dogs understand when they have done wrong and can learn from their mistakes. If a dog senses your anger or displeasure, it will take notice—unlike a cat, which understands but usually chooses to ignore you. It is up to the owner to let the dog know that it has done wrong, and the scolding must be clearly associated with the misbehavior. A puppy that has made a mess on the kitchen floor will not understand what it has done wrong if the scolding comes two hours after the fact.

***Facing page:* Dogs are willing students because they instinctively want to please their owners, but a dog will not learn unless the owner is firm and consistent.**

Early Training

Your puppy will need a lightweight collar and leash. Some puppies will object to a collar being placed around their necks and will try to remove it, but others won't be fazed by a collar at all. Make sure the collar is loose enough to slip two fingers underneath it, but not so loose that it will get caught on something.

Getting your puppy used to the leash may prove more difficult, so use the lightest weight leash you can find—a cat leash is perfect. Let your dog wander around the house with the leash on so that it becomes accustomed to it. A very young puppy should not be taken for walks because it risks infection and will tire easily. However, if you are housebreaking your dog you will need to take your dog outside. For safety's sake, you should keep the puppy on a leash when you take it outside to relieve itself. As soon as your puppy is old enough to go for a walk, teach it how to walk on a leash. From a young age encourage it to stay close by your side. A firm voice and a gentle tug on the leash should be enough to keep a puppy in line. Serious lessons on how to heel should wait until the puppy is about three and a half months old. If you train your puppy to walk on a leash at a young age, learning to heel will be much easier. Do not allow your puppy to chew on the leash while on a walk.

Part of a puppy's charm is its playful nature, but every owner will need some peace and quiet. A young puppy can be taught to go to its bed or box and stay there. Use a command like 'Go to sleep' or 'Bed' and if the puppy tries to leave its bed firmly tell it to 'Stay.' As in all training, the key is firmness and consistency. If your resolve weakens, puppy will know that it has the upper hand.

An offshoot of this lesson is teaching your puppy to stay by itself. The first time you leave your puppy alone it will bark—a habit which is likely to persist unless the dog is properly trained. To accustom your puppy to being alone, leave it in familiar surroundings. When it barks, make sure it is all right—that it is not asking to go outside—but don't give in and let the puppy get the best of you. Leave the puppy alone!

To keep your puppy from chewing on your belongings, first, make sure it has plenty of toys it can chew on. When your puppy does chew on something it should not, reprimand it by firmly telling it 'No' or give the command 'Drop it.' Then give the puppy one of its toys.

At top: This Airedale puppy is being taught to sit. *Above:* One of your puppy's first lessons will be learning to wear a leash and collar. Begin with a lightweight leash and collar, later switching to a heavier leash as the puppy grows. The local pet shop has a wide selection of leashes *(right)* suitable for your dog, from puppyhood to adulthood. *Facing page:* A Great Dane.

THE PICTORIAL GUIDE TO DOG CARE

At top: **A small class of Standard Poodle puppies learns how to sit.** *Center:* **The proper way to put on a choke collar. Note that the collar pulls from above the neck.** *Above:* **The wrong way to put on a choke collar. A collar worn this way can harm the dog.** *Facing page, above:* **This Poodle has mastered 'Stay' while on the leash and has progressed to the next part of the lesson — off the leash. The final part of the lesson is teaching the dog to stay while the owner moves out of sight.**

Simple Commands

The first commands to teach your puppy are sit, stay, come, heel and down. Keep training lessons short—about 10 minutes—as a puppy's attention span is not long. Train your puppy in an area free of distractions. Reward it with positive reinforcement—'Good Dog!'—when it obeys a command rather than scolding it when it does not obey. Lavish praise and a pat on the head or a scratch behind the ears will be much more effective than coaxing it with food. Master one lesson before moving on to the next command, and always use the same command. Don't confuse your puppy by alternating 'Come' with 'Come over here right now!'

SIT. Use a leash to train your dog to sit. Give the command 'Sit' and push down on the dog's hindquarters with your left hand, while pulling up on the leash with the right. If you pull up and push down at the same time, you will naturally ease your dog into a sitting position. Although dogs learn quickly, your dog will be puzzled at first. It will want to please, but won't know what you want so keep showing it how to sit. If you start to feel frustrated, you and your dog will both be better off to end the lesson for the time being. If you repeat the lesson every day, your dog will soon understand. Once your dog has obeyed the command to sit several times, take the leash off. It should now obey the command without the reinforcement from the leash. If not, go back to using the leash.

STAY. 'Stay' is a more difficult command. Using the leash again, begin your lesson by running through 'Sit.' With your dog in a sitting position, tell it to 'Stay.' Take up the slack in the leash to keep your dog in place. When the dog starts to move, firmly tell it 'NO.' Back away from the dog, repeating the command to stay. Be sure to maintain eye contact with your dog. As you back away slacken the leash. When the dog appears to understand, try giving the command as you walk around it. Eventually, try the lesson without the leash.

You can reinforce the 'Stay' command by using a hand signal—your hand raised in the air like a police officer directing traffic.

COME. When you call your dog's name, most of the time it will come bounding to your side. At times, however, it will be distracted and won't come running. The command 'Come' teaches your dog to come even when it does not want to.

Begin the lesson by giving your dog the command to stay. Walk away from it and then call it by name, along with the command 'Come.' You may have to give a little tug on the leash to show your dog that you really do want it to come to you. A gesture, such as a clap or slapping your hand against your thigh, will help

excite your dog into motion. When your dog does come to you, lavish it with praise—'What a wonderful dog! Sarah, you're such a good girl!' Make your dog want to come to you.

HEEL. Your dog should be taught to heel, both on and off the leash. This lesson will take longer to learn than the other commands and therefore requires more patience on your part. To train your dog to heel you will need a choke collar. For a small dog, you can use a choke collar made of nylon instead of metal. The choke collar should be about two inches longer than the dog's regular collar—it needs to be long enough to pull on and off over the dog's head. To use a choke collar, hold the collar by the rings, one above the other and drop the chain through the lower ring. Put the collar on so that it pulls from *above* the neck, not below. In this way, the chain will automatically loosen when you let up on the leash. The choke collar will not hurt your dog; it is designed to get your dog's attention by making it feel uncomfortable. Many people have the mistaken idea that a choke is harmful and therefore buy the one with the smallest links because they look less menacing. The reality is that the larger link chain collars are better for the dog.

Use the choke collar *only* for training and walking. If you leave the choke collar on your dog all the time, you run the risk of it getting caught on something. Choke collars also tend to discolor your dog's coat. In addition, you will need a sturdy leash, about six feet long, for training.

Your dog should walk beside you, with its right shoulder next to your left leg. Shorten the leash so that the dog stays near your side and tell it 'Heel' as you start walking. If it starts to pull away, jerk the leash while firmly repeating the command 'Heel!' Continue walking as you jerk the leash. The object is to make your dog walk by your side. Stopping and jerking does not give your dog a clear idea of what you want it to do. As you walk along, speak reassuringly to your dog—it will probably be confused.

When your dog is beginning to understand 'Heel,' teach it how to heel while turning. Right turns are easier to learn, so try them first. If it has trouble heeling while you turn, take a shorter grip on the leash to force it to move with you.

When your dog heels properly with a slack leash, it is time to try heeling without the leash. If your dog doesn't heel as it should without the leash, reprimand it sharply. If that fails, put the leash back on and run through the now familiar routine.

Heeling is more than your dog walking quietly by your side—it is walking by your side even though your dog encounters countless distractions—other dogs, fascinating smells, sticks and stones to pick up and passersby who coo, 'What an adorable dog.' A well trained dog ignores all distractions, no matter how

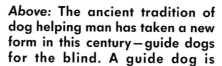
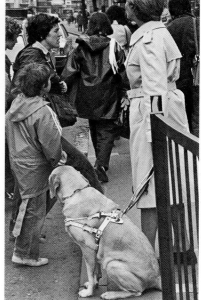

Above: **The ancient tradition of dog helping man has taken a new form in this century—guide dogs for the blind. A guide dog is trained to walk close by the side of its blind master, who directs the dog's movements through a rigid leather-covered loop attached to a harness. The guide dog leads its master around obstacles and stops at curbs so that the blind person can assess the height of the step. At stop lights, the dog pauses until there is a break in the flow of traffic.**

A blind person relies so completely on his or her guide dog that training must be rigorous and thorough. German Shepherds (known in Great Britain as Alsatians) are often used as guide dogs because the breed is highly intelligent and loyal. Golden Retrievers and Labrador Retrievers are also trained as guide dogs. Female dogs are used more frequently than males, but the temperament of the individual dog is the deciding factor in selecting a suitable dog.

fascinating. When your dog is doing well with heel, take it for a walk among people. If possible don't stop when people want to pet it, as this will only excite your dog. Keep walking when you see other dogs, and don't stop to let your dog sniff. Teach your dog to sit whenever you stop, whatever the reason—a traffic light, an interesting shop window, a chance encounter with a friend. Eventually, when you take your dog out on a crowded street it will sit politely by your side if and when you decide to stop.

DOWN. Start with your dog in the sit position. Then pull the front legs forward and push down on its shoulders as you give the command 'Down.' Alternative methods for putting the dog in the down position are: 1) From a sitting position, lift one front leg while gently pushing the opposite shoulder toward the raised leg. This forces the dog to lie down; or 2) Apply pressure on the choke chain by stepping on the leash with your foot. Release pressure as soon as the dog is down. Repeat several times until your dog associates the action with the word. Be sure to praise your dog when it stays in the down position.

Obedience School

Some owners find it helpful to enroll their dogs in obedience school. Although such classes may conjure up the image of a roomful of bad dogs, obedience schools are really more for the owner than the dog. Training a dog requires a certain amount of knowledge and discipline, and many first time dog owners don't know what to do when confronted with a rambunctious four-month-old puppy. The classes are taught by experienced dog handlers who will guide you and your dog through the intricacies of training.

To find a reputable dog school, check with your veterinarian or local humane society. Friends with dogs of their own who have successfully completed a class are another good source. Don't hesitate to check out the school before you enroll your dog. Ideally, the class should be limited to ten students. Talk with the trainer and/or watch a class. The dogs should be handled firmly, but not beaten into submission.

Training the Problem Dog

BITING DOGS. Most dogs bite out of fear. Since many dog bites are inflicted against children, when possible you can attempt to modify the behavior of children as well as the dog. Tell your children and the neighborhood children not to run up to the dog. They should never extend their fingers to the dog, but instead should show the dog a clinched fist. To help the dog overcome its fearful aggression, you need to desensitize the dog. If your dog always barks at and tries to bite strangers, you need to teach the dog not to be afraid. To do this, you will need a friend to help you. Have your helper face the dog from a safe distance

At top: A Labrador Retriever goes through guide dog training. German Shepherds are important members of the armed forces and are trained to assist on patrol *(center)* and to sniff out explosives and drugs *(above). Facing page:* Poodles are known for their trainability and, in addition to obedience training, can be taught to do a number of tricks.

A German Shorthaired Pointer combines the skills of a pointer with a retriever. Training involves teaching the dog to find the game (*at top*) and also retrieve it. *Above:* The occasional treat can provide positive reinforcement during training. Some dogs can even be trained to sit with a biscuit on the nose. If trainer and dog become too frustrated, a biscuit on the paw may be an easier trick to learn.

and reward non-aggressive behavior with praise or food. With each training session, reduce the distance between the dog and the feared object. Always reward good behavior with praise and punish bad behavior by ignoring the dog. Any sort of attention, even punishment by scolding, may reinforce the bad behavior.

SEPARATION ANXIETY. Some dogs have extreme reactions to being left alone. They bark and whine in your absence, chew objects to the point of destruction and urinate and defecate in the house. Most puppies experience some form of anxiety when first left alone, but in most cases they become used to being left alone. Avoid major problems by handling the situation when the dog is young. Having a regular routine helps to ease the problem. Every dog needs an area of its own, whether it is a dog run or a corner of the kitchen. Train your puppy to 'Go to sleep' at a natural time to do so—after eating or playing and put it in its special area. When you leave the puppy alone, it should be ready to sleep and will come to associate being left alone with going to sleep. To combat destructive chewing, give your dog plenty of distractions—rubber toys, rawhide chews. Don't draw attention to your departure with a lengthy farewell, instead leave with a quick and upbeat good-bye. Prior to leaving have a minimum amount of contact with your dog.

FEAR OF LOUD NOISES. Many dogs are frightened by loud noises—anything from vacuum cleaners and hair dryers to fireworks and thunder. You can help your dog overcome its fear by getting it accustomed to other loud noises. For example, drop a book on the floor and then speak to the dog reassuringly. With a young dog, at the first sign of fear, reassure it before the fear develops into a phobia, but be careful the reassurance doesn't become a positive reward in itself!

URINATING IN THE HOUSE. In some cases, the dog may be attempting to mask another scent, such as perfume or tobacco, so you will need to remove the source. In other cases, the problem may be hormonal. Male dogs mark their territory with urine, and a female dog uses her urine to tell males she is available. In these situations, your first approach should be to go through the steps for housebreaking again. If that fails, talk to your vet about neutering the animal. If you cannot determine the cause of the problem, consult your vet—improper elimination may have its roots in a physical disorder.

JUMPING UP. Dogs jump up because they are excited to see you. To break your dog of this bad habit, firmly tell it no and then give it the command 'Sit' or 'Down.' Go down to the dog's level and praise it and pet it. Praise your dog every time it greets you on all fours.

BEGGING. Reprimand your dog if it begs for food, and *never* give in and feed it from the dinner table. Feeding your dog before you eat will help eliminate the urge to beg for food from your dinner.

Training For Fun

When your dog has mastered the essential commands of sit, stay, come, heel and down, you can move on to other more amusing commands: fetch, give me your paw, roll over and the like. The principles for obedience training apply to any sort of training:

1. Keep the training sessions short.
2. Show your dog what you want it to do. Dogs don't speak English, so you need to manipulate them into the correct position.
3. Praise your dog when it performs the command.
4. Work on only one command at a time.

FETCH. Some dogs, especially retrievers, will naturally bring a thrown object back to their owners. Training reinforces this natural tendency, while teaching the dog that there is a proper time for everything. The untrained dog may have no problem with fetching a ball, but it may want to play fetch while you are trying to read the Sunday paper; conversely, it may decide to chew on the ball rather than return it to you when you throw it.

To teach a dog to fetch, throw a ball or stick and call out 'Fetch.' Your dog will naturally run after it. If the dog doesn't return with the object, command it to 'Come.' If the dog prefers romping around with its plaything, a long leash to pull the dog to you will come in handy. Shower your dog with praise when it returns. Tell it to 'Sit' and take the object from its mouth. If the dog resists your removing the object, grasp its upper jaw, telling it 'Let Go.' 'Fetch' is fun as well as useful because it a good way to give your dog the exercise it needs.

GIVE ME YOUR PAW. Begin the lesson by telling the dog to sit. Take one of your dog's paws (always use the same one) in your hand while repeating the command 'Give me your paw.' Dogs instinctively lift a paw during play so this action is not as strange as it may seem. With some dogs, a biscuit encourages the movement, but some will simply be distracted by the food. Be sure to reinforce the action with lavish praise.

ROLL OVER. Roll over is more difficult to learn. To teach your dog to roll over, tell it to lie down and then take it through the motions of rolling over while repeating 'Roll over.' Moving your hand in a circling motion provides a good visual command.

BISCUIT ON THE NOSE. A well-trained dog can be taught to sit with a biscuit on its nose. Tell your dog to sit, place a dog biscuit on its nose and firmly tell it to stay. At first, you will lose a few dog biscuits. Reprimand your dog if it refuses to stay and eats the biscuit. Reward the dog with the biscuit when it stays. In time, the dog will learn that it will get the dog biscuit if it sits still.

At top: Poodles are performers at heart and can be trained to leap over hurdles. *Center:* Exercising your dog before a training session will work off excess energy and make your dog more attentive. *Above:* Shannon, a Lab mix, eagerly returns the frisbee to her trainer, who rewards her with a pat on the head and an encouraging word.

Housing And Supplies

A Bed For Your Dog

All dogs need a place to call home. Dogs are territorial animals and a bed gives a dog a sense of security. The dog's bed is also a good place to send your dog when you want it to be quiet. Pet stores offer an array of beds for your dog, ranging from wicker baskets to plastic beds. Line the basket with a pad, old towel, soft rug or blanket. Some dogs will be satisfied with just the blanket. Large dogs enjoy sleeping on bean bag chairs, but be sure to buy the kind with a removable, washable cover.

Outdoor Kennels

Owners of large dogs often keep their dogs in pens or dog runs at night or during the day while they are away. The size of the pen depends on the size of the dog and how much time it will spend in the pen. The more space, the better. For a large dog (retriever size), the run should be at least 6 feet wide by 15 feet long by 6 feet high. It should be constructed of strong chainlink fence. As protection against the escape artist dog, you may want to bury boards around the bottom to prevent your dog from digging under the fence. As a base, use smooth stone that gently slopes toward a drain, making for easy cleaning with a hose.

The run should be equipped with a doghouse to protect your dog from the rain, snow, wind and cold. The doghouse should be large enough for your dog to stand or sleep in it comfortably and small enough for the dog's body heat to warm the structure. In cold-weather areas, you may want to insulate the dog house. The house should be raised a couple of inches from the ground as protection against dampness and insects. A hinged or removable roof will facilitate cleaning. After you've gone to the trouble of giving your dog a wonderful doghouse, don't be surprised if your dog sits in the rain instead of seeking the comfort of the doghouse. Nonetheless, your dog should have the house available; it may crawl inside when it gets bored with the rain.

Facing page: The Old English Sheepdog is a friendly and obedient dog, if given the necessary attention and training. Its heritage as a working dog is still very much a part of its personality, so these large dogs need plenty of space and exercise.

Carrying Case

Because many dogs are content to sit quietly in the back seat while traveling by car, dog carriers are primarily used for travel by air or rail. When traveling by air make sure that your case conforms to airline regulations. For the small dog or puppy, a case might be helpful for the occasional trip to the vet. Don't buy a carrier for a puppy if it will soon outgrow it. A cardboard box will see you through the visits to the vet. A wire cage also comes in handy for housebreaking or disciplining a puppy. (See the section on housebreaking.)

For those dogs that are somewhat boisterous in the car, a wire grille that confines the dog to the back of the car makes traveling more enjoyable for both of you.

Collars and Leashes

Your puppy's first collar should be lightweight, preferably one that can be adjusted as your puppy grows. Be sure to check the collar regularly and adjust the collar as needed. Puppies grow at an incredible rate! When your puppy is full grown, purchase a leather or nylon collar. A collar a half inch wide is fine for most dogs; larger breeds require a collar that is one to one and a half inches wide.

Leashes come in a wide array of lengths, styles and materials—rope, leather, nylon, cotton, chain. Large dogs obviously require a sturdy leash. When buying a leash, check the clip. A flimsy clip on an otherwise sturdy leash weakens the leash. Some leashes are equipped with an automatic reel, extending 15 to 30 feet, which lets your dog enjoy a good romp while you remain in control.

For your own peace of mind, purchase an identity tag. Imagine how you would feel if your dog somehow got lost and had no source of identification. Of course you must follow all applicable licensing laws of your municipality, which will also aid in your dog's recovery in the event of its loss.

At top: Airlines have strict regulations governing the size and type of carrier you may use to transport your dog. *Above:* A wicker basket is a favorite bed for many dogs, although some dogs are quite content with a blanket on the floor. Pet doors give your dog the best of both worlds—access to the backyard and the comforts of the living room. *Right:* A dog run lets your dog move about freely in the open, while giving you peace of mind that your dog is secure. The size of the run should be based on the size of the breed. The more space you can provide the better. *Facing page:* In some communities, the humane society offers a tattooing service—a permanent method of identifying your dog. Unlike an ID tag, a tattoo will never fall off a collar and get lost.

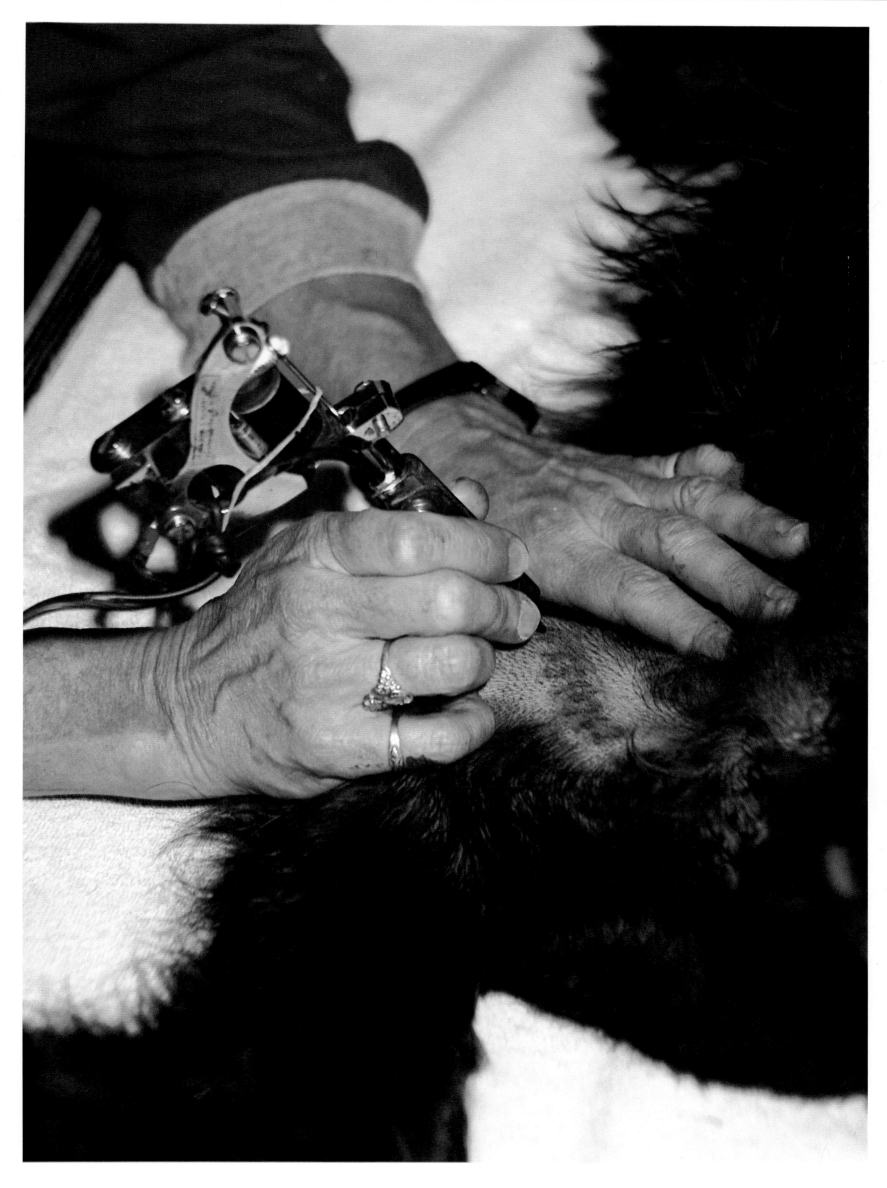

Breeding Your Dog

Raising puppies takes a great deal of time, space and energy. It is not a profit-making venture and should not be undertaken lightly. If you want to breed your dog, an experienced, reputable breeder can help you find a mate for your dog, or, at the very least, teach you the principles of dog breeding. Far too many unwanted puppies are produced by irresponsible breeders. Professional breeders despair over the number of 'amateurs' who breed their dogs, claiming careless breeding pollutes the gene pool. To the amateur, this point of view may seem to contradict the system of free enterprise, not to mention an infringement of one's personal rights. Unfortunately, there is some truth to the professionals' claim. Many people do see breeding as an opportunity to make money when a breed becomes popular. The end result is that little thought is given to selecting males and females that complement each other. Instead of looking at the bloodline these irresponsible breeders look at the bottom line. Irresponsible breeding practices can lead to health or temperament problems. Carelessly bred Golden Retrievers, an extremely popular breed right now, may exhibit rage syndrome. These normally sweet-dispositioned dogs are difficult to train and may even attack other dogs as well as people, including their masters. If you do plan on breeding your dog, make sure you know what you are doing. If you never intend to breed her, have her spayed.

The first step in breeding your dog is to find a suitable mate. Your local breed society can supply you with a list of available studs. Finding an appropriate male means studying his pedigree and conformation. The pedigree should be free from any inherited health problems, such as eye disorders or hip dysplasia. Look for a dog that best typifies the breed standard, and, above all, avoid one that has the same faults as your female. If your female's head is too narrow for the standard, don't breed her with a male that also has a narrow head. The goal is to eliminate the weaknesses in your dog's bloodline. In order to find the ideal male, you may have to look outside your community.

Your female needs to be mature enough to handle the physical and mental demands of a litter. Most dogs stop growing at about a year, although the larger breeds need another six months or so to fill out completely. It is a good practice

***Facing page:* A pair of English Springer Spaniels and their puppy. Breeding dogs is fun, but is more work than most people realize.**

At top: Two Siberian Huskies out for walk with their owners. ***Above:*** A dog and her litter. The puppies will soon be old enough to leave their mother.

to let your dog go through a normal heat before you breed her. When you decide that your female is old enough, take her to the vet to be checked for worms and for booster shots before she goes into heat.

Watch for the signs that tell you your dog is in heat—a swelling of the vulva and a clear discharge that becomes bloody. Some dogs show almost no external signs, in which case your vet may have to determine the stage of her cycle. The best time to breed your dog is between nine and 14 days after the beginning of the discharge. Some breeders recommend the tenth day; others prefer the twelfth day. After the mating, keep your female dog away from other males. Until she is out of heat, she can still conceive.

Caring For Your Pregnant Dog

When your dog is out of heat, treat her normally. About the fifth week after mating, you should be able to tell by her body shape if she is pregnant. At this time, your vet will recommend a whelping diet. There are good, high protein commercial foods available. At the sixth or seventh week, she will need more food, and your vet may suggest that you feed her smaller but more frequent meals. Reduce exercise around the seventh week. Regular, short walks are a good idea, but don't let her get involved in rough and tumble play. Make sure she does not become overtired.

The gestation period is usually 63 days, although puppies can arrive a week early or late. A few weeks before the puppies are due, introduce your dog to a whelping box. If you wait and show her the box shortly before whelping, she will be reluctant to deliver her puppies in an unfamiliar place and will likely have already selected a spot. You can make the box yourself or purchase one. Place the box in a draft-free area and line it with a thick layer of newspapers covered with a blanket. The whelping box should be large enough for your dog to lie down and stretch out but not so large that the puppies will wander too far and become chilled. Puppies' systems do not regulate heat well, so they need their mother's body heat to keep them warm. Keep the temperature of the box between 70 and 80 degrees Fahrenheit. It may be necessary to use a supplemental heat source, such as a heat lamp. If so, don't place the lamps too close to the box, as the lamps can cause overheating or even burns. An alternative is to keep the room temperature high.

If you have a long-haired dog, you may want to trim the hair around the nipples before whelping to make it easier for the puppies to nurse.

The Birth

In most cases, a female will handle birth without assistance. Only you should be present at whelping, as a number of people will distress her. Plan on keeping your distance, although a few dogs like reassurance from their owners.

Your dog will let you know when she is ready to deliver. She will become restless and wander in and out of her box. She will frantically rearrange her bedding. When she starts panting heavily and contractions are visible, she is in labor. When the first puppy enters the pelvis, the contractions become stronger, longer and more frequent. Soon the first puppy will appear and will be pushed out with the contractions.

When the first puppy is out, the mother should open the amniotic sac with her teeth and chew off the umbilical cord. She will lick the puppy, which cleans it and stimulates breathing. The newborn puppy will seek out a nipple and begin to suck, promoting the milk supply. The placenta may come out with the puppy, or it may follow up to 15 minutes later. Your dog will probably eat the placenta, and this is fine, as it encourages labor. Be sure the number of placentas expelled agrees with the number of puppies delivered. Sometimes the placenta for one puppy will come out with the next puppy delivered.

Puppies generally arrive in half hour intervals, although the time between the first and second is generally longer than the time between the other puppies. If your dog has not delivered her second puppy after two hours, call your veterinarian. The length of labor depends on the number of puppies, typically lasting no more than eight hours. Large litters (12 to 14 puppies) take more time of course, and the mother may take a break in the middle. Experienced females will deliver more quickly than the first-time mother.

At top: **A Tibetan Terrier with her puppies.** ***Above:*** **A puppy partakes of a hearty meal of Canine Growth, a premium dog food made especially for puppies, as well as for pregnant and nursing dogs.**

Sometimes the mother does not know how to deal with the newborn puppies, and you will have to help her. To sever the umbilical cord, firmly pinch the cord closed in the middle with your fingers or a pliers, and then cut the cord a few inches from the puppy's belly using a scissors. Tying the cord first with stout button thread helps prevent bleeding. Clear the membranes from the puppy's nose and mouth and then rub it briskly with a warm towel to stimulate breathing. Don't clean the puppy completely—some dogs will reject a puppy that has been handled too much by the owner. Just do what is necessary and return the puppy to its mother.

In rare instances, puppies have to be delivered by Caesarean section. The vet will give your dog a general anaesthetic, make an incision in the midline of her flank, and then remove the puppies from the uterus and stitch up the incision. You will probably be able to take the dog and her puppies home about two hours after the operation. Be sure to check the incision several times a day and call your vet immediately if you notice anything unusual.

After Delivery

Following whelping, your dog may have a green or bloody discharge for 24 hours, although the discharge can last up to a week after the birth of a large litter. Bathe the area with an antiseptic. Your dog may also vomit or have diarrhea.

Continue to feed your dog with the same high quality whelping diet you fed her during the pregnancy. While she is nursing, she will require up to three times as much food as she normally eats.

If your dog's nipples become red and swollen, consult your veterinarian. This condition is called mastitis. The vet may advise you to bathe the area in warm water and then draw off excess milk by squeezing and releasing the nipple. Often the condition corrects itself when the puppies start nursing more.

Eclampsia is a more serious condition. Caused by a calcium deficiency, the problem usually occurs just before whelping or in the month following. Dogs that have large litters and have lots of milk are prone to eclampsia. Symptoms include restlessness, panting and whining. As the condition progresses, the dog becomes stiff and uncoordinated. If not treated, she will collapse with convulsions and die. This condition warrants emergency treatment. Your vet will give the dog a calcium injection.

Caring For Newborn Puppies

Though blind, deaf and seemingly helpless, a puppy has an amazing sense of smell that helps it seek out its mother's milk. During the first few days of its life, a puppy receives from its mother's milk the protective antibodies that will take it through the first two months. At about 10 to 14 days, its eyes open, but it will take another seven days before it can focus. Hearing begins to work when the ear canals open, between 13 and 17 days. For the first few weeks, a puppy depends completely on its mother. She cleans and feeds it and even licks away the urine and feces to keep the whelping box clean.

When the puppies are about a month old, you can begin to wean them from their mother's milk. The easiest way to wean a puppy is to use a high quality commercial puppy food. Add enough hot water to create a lukewarm, thin

At top: Airedale puppies nursing. The mother's milk gives the puppies passive immunity against disease until they are old enough to be vaccinated. *Above:* The mother dog takes complete care of her newborn puppies during the first few weeks. *Right:* A puppy may need to be hand-fed if the mother has a large litter and cannot adequately nurse all her puppies. *Facing page, top:* Exercise and training begins at an early age. *Facing page, center:* A Collie and her puppy. *Facing page, below:* A litter of Golden Retriever puppies has adopted a kitten as one of its own.

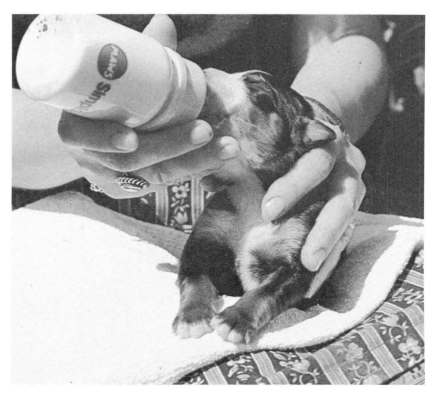

mush. Feed the puppies in a large, shallow dish and encourage them to eat by placing a small bit of food on each puppy's nose. The puppies will lick their noses and will be enticed into trying more of the delicious mixture. Typically, during the first few days of weaning, puppies walk through their food in addition to eating it, so be sure to wipe them off after every meal. Food left on the skin can lead to dermatitis. Gradually decrease the amount of water added to the dry food. By six weeks, puppies should be almost if not completely weaned. Once weaned, the growing puppy should be fed four times a day.

Hand-feeding Puppies

If the litter is large, the mother cannot feed all her puppies, so some will have to be hand-fed. Some puppies are simply born weaker and they, too, will need your attention. A weak puppy feels damp and limp. In the whelping box it will crawl around and whimper, and, if not watched carefully will crawl off to a corner, where it stays, becoming weaker and weaker.

To hand-feed a puppy, you will need a nursing bottle designed especially for pets or a baby bottle for premature babies. Don't use eye droppers because they force in too much air. Your vet will tell you what to feed the puppy. Add the mixture and heat it to 100.4 degrees Fahrenheit. Heat the bottle by placing it in a bowl of boiling water or microwave it. Be sure to test the formula on your wrist to see that it is not too hot. To feed the puppy, guide the bottle nipple into its mouth while supporting its rib cage. Let its legs move freely in the 'kneading' reflex. After feeding you will need to stimulate its bowel and bladder. Gently massage the puppy's abdomen and wipe the anal area clean with a damp tissue.

In some cases, the hand-fed puppy must not be returned to the mother because she will reject it. With a high-strung dog, the human smell on the puppy will cause her to lick it frantically and, in extreme cases, kill it. After feeding a puppy, return it to her and carefully but discreetly watch her reaction.

Hand-fed puppies can be weaned at an earlier age than their siblings. At about two and a half weeks, try feeding in a saucer instead of the bottle. As the puppy learns to eat out of the saucer, make sure it is getting enough to eat or the weak puppy may suffer a setback.

Worming and Shots

Many breeders routinely take the puppies to the vet for the first of their inoculations when they are six or seven weeks old. This is also a good time to check for worms. Many puppies have roundworms that are passed to them from their mothers.

Seven weeks is the best time for the puppies to find a new home. After putting in an enormous amount of time, energy and money into rearing your puppies, you will want the puppies to go to a good home. Don't hesitate to ask the prospective owner about himself and what sort of home the puppy will have.

Showing Your Dog

The term 'dog show' generally refers to a bench competition, which judges the dog on the basis of appearance, physique, bearing and temperament according to the breed standard—a description of a perfect specimen of the breed. A standard is quite detailed, discussing everything from the color of the nose to the size of the tail, from how the dog moves to its expression. A deviation from the standard is considered a fault. Thus, a fault could be physical, such as legs that are too long, or temperamental, such as hostility or timidity in the ring. The standard serves as a guide for judges and breeders alike.

The first dog shows were held in England in the 1830s. One authority has suggested that these low-key events were a result of the ban on dog fighting and bull baiting. Following the ban, dog fanciers channeled their competitive energies in a less barbarous direction, and dog shows were born in the local pubs and taverns. The first official dog show took place at Newcastle-upon-Tyne, England in 1859. Dog clubs developed because judges and breeders disagreed over what constituted a winning dog. The clubs established the standards governing the breeds.

Today, the Westminster Dog Show, in New York is the most prestigious championship dog show in the United States. Crufts, established in 1886, is the major show in England. Entry to these shows is limited to dogs that have won the required certificates at other championship shows.

Above: A group of show Salukis. *Facing page:* A Poodle puppy at a dog show undergoes a few last minute preparations.

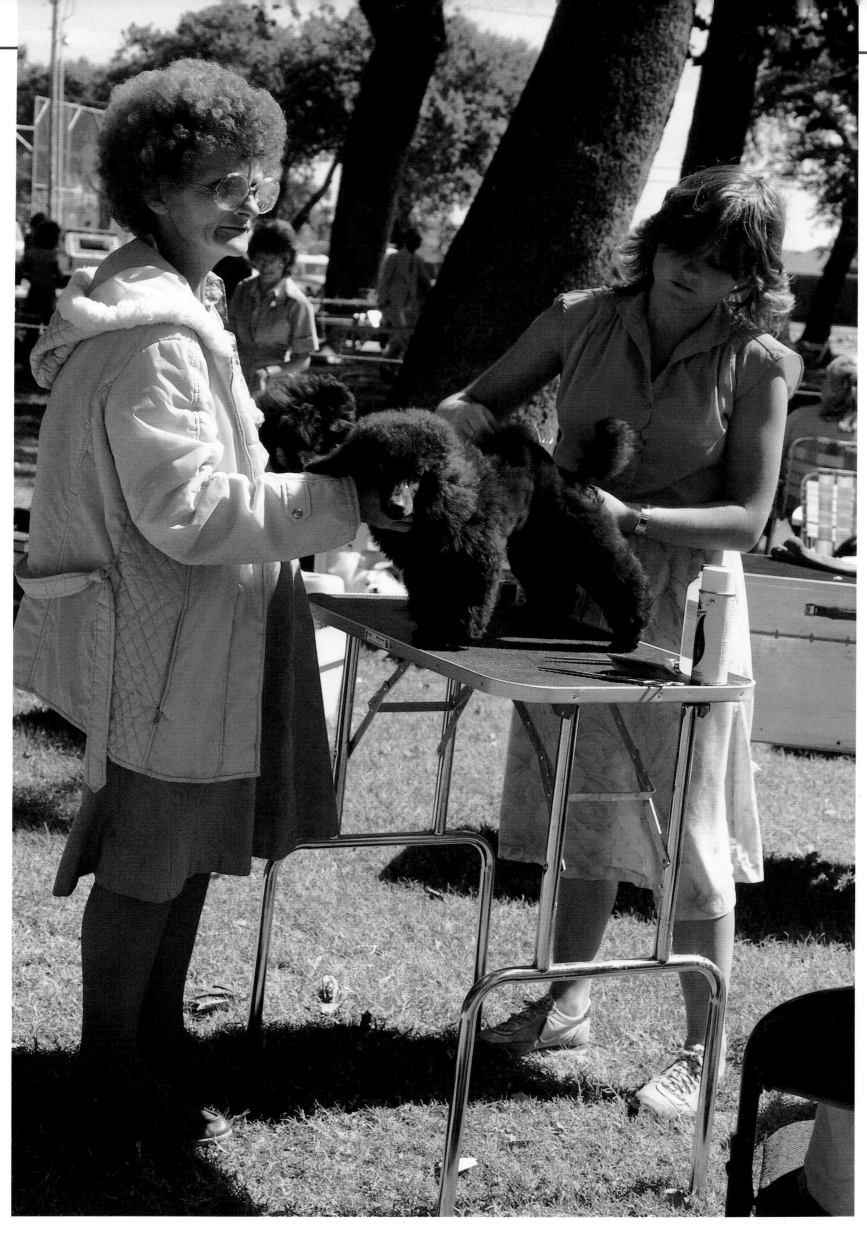

If you would like to enter your pedigreed dog in a dog show, your local breed society can advise you about upcoming shows and the proper procedure for entering. Match shows are less intense forms of competition, as they do not award championship points and are therefore a good starting point for the amateur dog handler. Unofficial shows are also open to mongrels.

Championship shows are divided into classes, first by breed and then by age and handicap, such as Puppy, Novice, Bred-by-Exhibitor and so on. Dogs and bitches are judged separately in each class, and then the first prize winners compete against each other, with the winner of each sex awarded 'Winners Dog' or 'Winners Bitch.' These dogs compete against any champions entered in the show and a 'Best-of-Breed' and 'Best of Opposite Sex' are selected.

If you enter your dog in a show, you will need to bring along supplies: grooming equipment; the dog's bed; drinking bowl and bottle of water (in case water is not readily available); food and feeding bowl; benching chain (to secure the dog to its stall); show leash, usually nylon or leather; and dog treats.

In addition to bench shows, dogs can compete in obedience, field and sheep dog trials. At an obedience trial, dogs (all breeds can compete against each other) are judged on ability to perform a series of exercises, including heel on leash, free heel, retrieve on flat or over high jump and scent discrimination. Typically, German Shepherds, Golden Retrievers and Labrador Retrievers excel at this type of competition.

Field trials test the ability of hunting dogs to perform the tasks for which the breeds were developed. The competition simulates actual hunting conditions.

Sheep dog trials pit working sheep dogs against each other. Dogs round up sheep and perform other herding operations, usually on a whistle command. For someone who has never seen a sheep dog in action these are truly fascinating competitions to watch.

At top: An illustration of a Mastiff at the second annual Westminster Kennel Club Dog Show in 1878. *Above:* Grand Bleus de Gascogne, a hound breed native to France, ready for the ring. *Right:* A prize-winning Saluki, one of the group pictured on page 120. *Facing page, above:* This diagram shows what a judge looks for when evaluating a dog. *Facing page, below:* A Basset Hound being gaited in the ring. One of the most important aspects of a dog's performance at a show is the way it moves. The expert handler makes this task seem easy, but it is much harder than it looks. The handler must give the dog enough space and freedom to move correctly, while giving himself enough room to move without impeding the dog. The handler also has the responsibility of selecting the route for the run, which involves looking for a clean path, free of any bumps that might interfere with the dog's gait.

THE PICTORIAL GUIDE TO DOG CARE

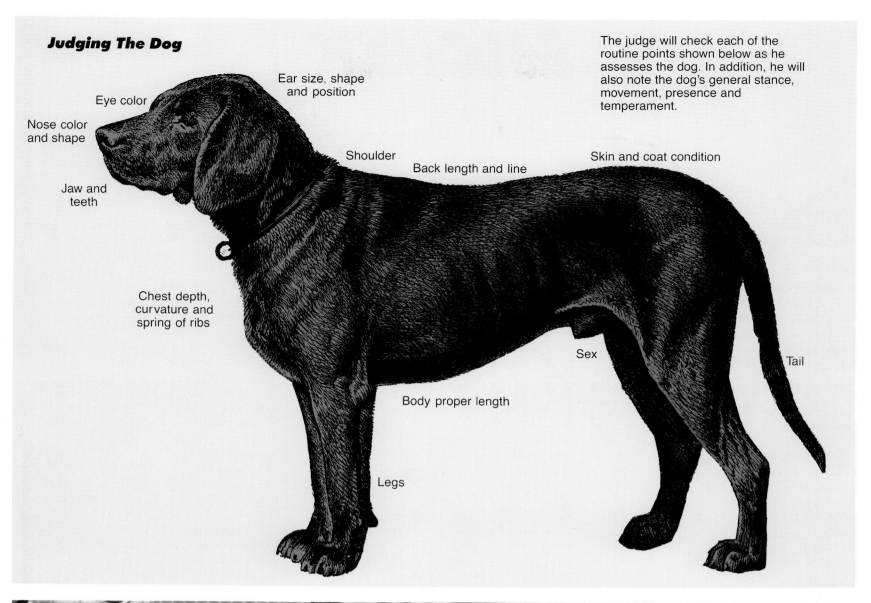

Judging The Dog

The judge will check each of the routine points shown below as he assesses the dog. In addition, he will also note the dog's general stance, movement, presence and temperament.

Nose color and shape

Eye color

Ear size, shape and position

Jaw and teeth

Shoulder

Back length and line

Skin and coat condition

Chest depth, curvature and spring of ribs

Sex

Tail

Body proper length

Legs

Index

F

False pregnancy 66
Fat 44, 62, 64
Fatigue 44, 48, 64
Fear of loud noises 108
Feeding 44-49, 50
   bowls *46*, 48
   puppies 38, 40, *40*
Fetch 48, *76*, 96, *98*, 109, *109*
Fever 54, 56, 68, 70, 94
Field trials 14, 122
First aid 92-95
Flat-coated Retriever 14, 16
Fleas 41, 72-74, *74*, 76-77, 86
Fluid therapy 62, 68
French Bulldog 28
Frothing at the mouth 94

G

Gagging 54
Generalized PRA 58-59
German Shepherd 22, *22, 50, 60, 105-106*, 122
German Shorthaired Pointer 14, *15, 108*
Giant Schnauzer 20
Glaucoma 56, 58
Golden Retriever 14, 16, 58-59, 60, *63*, 84, *105, 119*, 122
Gontjaja *20*
Gordon Setter 14, 16
Grand Bleu de Gascogne 122
Great Britain 24-25
Great Dane 8, 20-21, 34, 88, *103*
Great Pyrenees 21, *54*
Greyhound 8, *8*, 18-19
Grooming 50, 82-85, *84*, 90
Guide dogs 105, *105-106*
Gums 78, 95
Guy Mannering 25

H

Hair loss 74
Harrier 18-19
Haw *see* Third eyelid
Head 60, 74
Hearing, loss of *see* Deafness
Heart 64, *64*, 77
   disorders 46, 56, 64, 74, 88
Heartworm 77
Heat 116
Heatstroke 94
Heel 100, 102, 104-105
Hepatitis *56*, 76
   see also Infectious canine hepatitis
Herding dogs 22
Herodotus 8
Hip 60
Hip dysplasia 60-62, 114
Hock joints 62
Hookworms 64, 72, 77
Hormone therapy 66
Hounds 18-19
Housebreaking 38, *38*, 108
Hubert, Saint 10
Hunting dogs 6, *8*, 14-16, *48*
Hypoglycemic coma 66

I

IAMS *40*
Ibizan Hound 18

Illness, signs of 50
Immune system 68
Immunotherapy 90
Infection 54, 60, 62-64, 80, 94
Infectious canine hepatitis 40, 68
Insulin 64
Intelligence 100
Intestines 41, 54, 76
Irish Setter *2-3*, 14, 59, *63*
Irish Terrier 25
Irish Water Spaniel 14
Irish Wolfhound 18, 19
Italian Greyhound 26

J

Japanese Chin 26
Jaundice 70
Jaw 70
Jogging 96

K

Kennel cough 40, 56, 70
Kennels 110
Keratitis 56
Kerry Blue Terrier *24*, 25
Kidney disease 62, 64, 88, 90
Kidney failure 54, 62, 88
Kidneys *62*, 63-64, 70
King Charles Spaniel 26, 64
Knee 62
Knights of Rhodes 10
Komondor 21
Kuvasz 21, *21*

L

Labrador Retriever 14, 16, *17*, 33, *54*, 59-60, 84, 88, *105-106*, 122
Lakeland Terrier 25
Lameness 60, 74, 95
Laryngitis 56
Larynx 56, *56*
Laxative 54
Leash 102, *102*, 104, 105, 109, 112
Leptospirosis 40, 62, 68, 70
Lhasa Apso 28
Lice 72, 74
Limping 60, 88
Listlessness 44, 68, 70, 76, 77
Liver *62*, 54, 70, 88, 90
Lung disease 46, 56
Lungs *56*, 76, 77
Lyme disease 74

M

Maltese 26, *26*, 84
Manchester Terrier 25
Mange 74
Mastiff 8, 10, 20, *122*
Mastitis 118
Medication, administering 66, 94, *95*
Metabolic disorders 46
Mexican Hairless 26
Mexico 10
Mineral deficiencies 64
Minerals 44, 46
Miniature Pinscher 26
Miniature Poodle *see* Poodle, Miniature
Miniature Schnauzer *see* Schnauzer

Mixed breed 30, *31*, 33
Mouth 64
   ulcers 62, 70
Moving an injured dog *94*, 95
Muscle disorders 46
Muzzle 95

N

Nail care 80
Neapolitan Mastiff *8*
Neolithic Age 6
Nerves *66*
Neutering 30
Newcastle-upon-Tyne, England 120
Newfoundland 21, *21*, 82
Nictating membrane *see* Third eyelid
Nineveh 8
Norwich Terrier 33
Nose 50
   discharge from 56, 70
Nutritional deficiencies 62

O

Obedience school 106
Obedience trials 122
Obesity 46, 48, *48*, 64
OFA *see* Orthopedic Foundation of America
Old English Sheepdog 22, 82, 84, *111*
Older dogs 56, 88-90
Orthopedic Foundation of America (OFA) 62
Osteoarthritis 62
Osteochondritis dissecans 60
Osteoporosis 62
Otter Hound 18, *18*, 19
Ovaries, removal of 66

P

Pancreas 64
Panting 94, 118
Papillon 26, *47*
Paralysis 68, 70
Parasites 72-77, *74, 76*, 94
Parvovirus 40, 54, 68, 70
Passive immunity 40, 118
Pekingese 26, 56
Periodontal disease 78, 88
Peru 10
Pet door 112
Pharaoh Hound 18
Pharynx *56*
'Pink eye' *see* Conjunctivitis
Placenta 77, 117
Play 98
Pneumonia 76
Pointer 14, 16
Poisons, poisoning 54, 62, 64, 92
Pomeranian 26
Pompeii 10
Poodles 59, 64
   Miniature 28, *29, 84*, 121
   Standard 28, *75, 104-105, 107, 109*
   Toy 26
Powder Puff 26
PRA *see* Progressive retinal atrophy
Prince Charles Spaniel 26
Progressive retinal atrophy (PRA) 58-59
Prostate 54, 88
Protein 44, 62
Pug 26, *27*, 56

Page 125: A trainer uses a hand signal to reinforce the verbal command to stay. *Overleaf:* The special bond that exists between a girl and her Boxer allows for gentle 'roughhousing.'